FREE DVD  FREE DVD

Essential Test Tips DVD from Trivium Test Prep

Dear Customer,

Thank you for purchasing from Trivium Test Prep! Whether you're looking to join the military, get into college, or advance your career, we're honored to be a part of your journey.

To show our appreciation (and to help you relieve a little of that test-prep stress), we're offering a **FREE** *AFOQT Essential Test Tips DVD* by Trivium Test Prep. Our DVD includes 35 test preparation strategies that will help keep you calm and collected before and during your big exam. All we ask is that you email us your feedback and describe your experience with our product. Amazing, awful, or just so-so: we want to hear what you have to say!

To receive your **FREE** *AFOQT Essential Test Tips DVD*, please email us at 5star@triviumtestprep. com. Include "Free 5 Star" in the subject line and the following information in your email:

1. The title of the product you purchased.

2. Your rating from 1 – 5 (with 5 being the best).

3. Your feedback about the product, including how our materials helped you meet your goals and ways in which we can improve our products.

4. Your full name and shipping address so we can send your **FREE** *AFOQT Essential Test Tips DVD*.

If you have any questions or concerns please feel free to contact us directly at 5star@triviumtestprep.com.

Thank you, and good luck with your studies!

AFOQT Practice Test Book

AFOQT Prep Book with Over 500 Practice Questions for the Air Force Officer Qualifying Test

TABLE OF CONTENTS

INTRODUCTION

C ongratulations on choosing to take the Air Force Officer Qualifying Test (AFOQT)! By purchasing this book, you've taken an important step on your path to joining the military.

This guide will provide you with a detailed overview of the AFOQT, so you know exactly what to expect on exam day. We'll take you through all the concepts covered on the exam and give you the opportunity to test your knowledge with practice questions. Even if it's been a while since you last took a major exam, don't worry; we'll make sure you're more than ready!

WHAT IS THE AFOQT?

Under the purview of the US Air Force, the AFOQT is a comprehensive exam used to measure aptitudes of candidates aspiring to enter the Air Force as an officer. This exam assesses candidates for acceptance into one of the Air Force commissioning programs. These programs include the Air Force Military Academy, Air Force Officer Training School (OTS), and the Air Force Reserve Officer Training Corps (Air Force ROTC). Results from this exam also determine a candidate's qualification for attendance to pilot and navigator training courses as well as nonaviation officer positions.

The AFOQT, written by several subject matter experts and revised in 2015, ensures the US Air Force recruits candidates that possess certain knowledge to meet the fundamental, rigid standards required of the modern and technical positions they will encounter as Air Force commissioned officers.

Only high school students applying for attendance in the US Air Force Military Academy, college students enrolled in their university ROTC program, and college graduates with bachelor's degrees are considered eligible to take the AFOQT.

WHAT'S ON THE AFOQT?

The AFOQT is broken down into twelve subtests. The entire exam is multiple choice, providing four or five possible answers with one being the correct or best answer. The exam is scored based on the total number of questions answered correctly. Therefore, test-takers are not penalized for guessing. Prior to starting some of the subtests, you may have the opportunity to answer some practice questions to ensure you understand what you are supposed to do. The exam itself requires three hours and thirty-six minutes; however, be prepared to allow at least five hours to account for administrative instruction, time between subtests, and two scheduled breaks.

Candidates must complete all subtests of the AFOQT, even if they are not applying to attend the pilot and navigator training courses. The subtests, approximate number of questions in each subtest, and the time allowed are shown in the following table.

What's on the AFOQT?

SUBTEST	APPROXIMATE NUMBER OF QUESTIONS	TIME LIMIT
1. Verbal Analogies	25	8 minutes
2. Arithmetic Reasoning	25	29 minutes
3. Word Knowledge	25	5 minutes
4. Math Knowledge	25	22 minutes
5. Reading Comprehension	25	38 minutes
6. Situational Judgment Test	50	35 minutes
7. Self-Description Inventory	220	40 minutes
8. Physical Science	20	10 minutes
9. Table Reading	40	7 minutes
10. Instrument Comprehension	25	5 minutes
11. Block Counting	30	4.5 minutes
12. Aviation Information	20	8 minutes
Total	530 multiple-choice questions	3 hours, 31 minutes

VERBAL ANALOGIES: tests your knowledge of the relationship between words.

ARITHMETIC REASONING: asks you to solve mathematical word problems using basic arithmetic equations, ratios, and statistics.

WORD KNOWLEDGE: assesses your understanding of antonyms, synonyms, and the meaning of words (vocabulary).

MATH KNOWLEDGE: asks you to calculate math equations using geometric and algebraic properties in addition to basic addition, subtraction, multiplication, and division.

READING COMPREHENSION: gauges your comprehension of written passages.

SITUATIONAL JUDGMENT TEST: examines your responses to decision-making situations junior officers typically encounter.

SELF-DESCRIPTION INVENTORY: evaluates your individual character traits and attitudes using a personality test.

PHYSICAL SCIENCE: explores the scope of your high school-level chemistry, physics, and Earth science knowledge.

TABLE READING: asks you to identify values provided in a table or graph as rapidly as possible.

INSTRUMENT COMPREHENSION: assesses your ability to recognize the response of an aircraft from graphics depicting instrument panel indicators.

Block Counting: provides a three-dimensional figure and asks you to count the number of blocks adjacent to or touching the block in question.

Aviation Information: tests your knowledge of aviation terminology and concepts, including the flight physics of fixed and rotary aircraft.

How Is the AFOQT Scored?

Each subtest score is quantified in a percentile ranking between 0 and 99 percent. This ranking is relative to your score ranked against other candidates who took the same subtest. After each subtest is computed, certain subtest scores are combined to correlate into a composite score for one of six separate categories: Verbal, Quantitative (Math), Academic Aptitude, Pilot, Combat Systems Operator (CSO), and Air Battle Manager (ABM). The Situational Judgment test is its own composite score category. While all six composite scores are used to determine eligibility for pilot and other aviation training courses, only the Verbal, Academic Aptitude, Situational Judgment, and Quantitative (Math) categories are used for nonaviation candidates. Due to the concentrated skill required for pilot and CSO positions, candidates must score higher in all categories to be eligible for attendance in the aviation training courses. The following covers how to attain a composite score for each category.

Verbal

To become an Air Force officer in any nonaviation position, you must score at least 15 in this subtest. The composite score for this category is a combination of Verbal Analogies, Word Knowledge, and Reading Comprehension. This category identifies candidates with strong understanding of language, grammar, and literature.

Quantitative

To become an Air Force officer in any nonaviation position, you must score at least 10 in this subtest. The composite score for this category is a combination of Arithmetic Reasoning and Math Knowledge. This category identifies candidates with a strong mathematical background understanding formulas, proportions, and ratios.

Academic Aptitude

The composite score for this category is a combination of Verbal Analogies, Arithmetic Reasoning, Word Knowledge, and Math Knowledge. This category identifies candidates with a broad academic knowledge. There is no minimum score in this category to be eligible to become an Air Force officer.

Pilot

The composite score for this category is a combination of Math Knowledge, Table Reading, Instrument Comprehension, and Aviation Information. This category identifies those candidates with particular talent in understanding aviation concepts, analyzing aeronautical charts, and possessing a quick response to surroundings. Candidates applying to become a pilot must score a minimum of 25 in this category. Candidates applying to become a CSO must score a minimum of 10 in this category. This category is not considered if applying to a nonaviation training course.

CSO

The composite score for this category is a combination of Word Knowledge, Math Knowledge, Table Reading, and Block Counting. This category identifies those candidates with technical aptitude in spatial ability coupled with verbal skill. Candidates applying to become a pilot must score a minimum of 10 in this category. Candidates applying to become a CSO must score a minimum of 25 in this category. There is no minimum score in this category if applying to a nonaviation training course.

Although the minimum Pilot and CSO composite scores for pilot and other aviation training course candidates are 25 and 10, respectively, candidates must attain a combined total composite score of 50 from the Pilot and CSO categories.

ABM

The composite score for this category is a combination of Verbal Analogies, Math Knowledge, Table Reading, Instrument Comprehension, Block Counting, and Aviation Information. This category identifies those candidates with particular technical competence in spatial ability, analyzing aeronautical charts, ability to recognize aircraft attitude, and verbal aptitude. There is no minimum score in this category to be eligible to become an Air Force officer.

Situational Judgment

The score for this category is taken from the Situational Judgment test. There is no minimum score in this category to be eligible to become an Air Force officer.

Although there is no minimum score for certain composite categories, the Air Force balances recruitment quotas by selecting candidates who attain the highest scores on the AFOQT. It is in your best interest to prepare for this test by studying and completing practice sample exam questions, especially in subtests that are not your strongest areas.

RETAKING THE AFOQT

The AFOQT may be taken twice in your lifetime. The retake exam must be taken after 180 days from the date of the initial exam. The most recent AFOQT score is used, not the highest score between the two exams. The AFOQT score is valid for life; however, the Air Force has a maximum age requirement at time of commissioning.

HOW IS THE AFOQT ADMINISTERED?

If you are ready to take the AFOQT, contact your local recruiter. Your officer recruiter will determine your initial eligibility to apply for officer schooling or to join the Air Force as an officer and schedule you for the AFOQT.

On the day of the exam, you will need to bring valid photo identification. Testing materials are provided by the test proctor. Calculators are not allowed. Personal breaks are scheduled by the proctor. The proctor will provide all instructions for taking the exam, such as when to start and stop, and will allow practice questions as applicable. During the practice questions, the proctor cannot provide information on the question, possible answers, or test-taking strategies.

GETTING TO KNOW THE UNITED STATES AIR FORCE

The US Air Force is tasked with missions to provide the global air support through superior air power for intelligence gathering, surveillance, and reconnaissance. The Air Force allows the United States to swiftly respond to threats and protect our national interests worldwide. The Air Force also leads the space and missile program, requiring various positions from combat crew operators to astronauts.

The rank structure of the Air Force consists of enlisted and officers, and it is similar to that of the US Army. The AFOQT only applies to individuals pursuing a career as a US Air Force officer. The US Air Force offers officer careers in the following fields: aviation, computer science, space command, munitions, command and control, intelligence, health, operations support, logistics, and more. Once you are determined to be qualified for a career field, the Air Force provides you with the training necessary to carry out the duties and responsibilities.

THE MILITARY RECRUITMENT PROCESS

As stated before, passing the AFOQT is just one requirement to qualify for military service as an officer in the US Air Force. You may contact your local recruiter through your high school counselor or college adviser, or visit your local military recruitment center.

Once you contact your local recruiter, he or she will meet with you at the recruiting office, your school, or your home. During this meeting, the recruiter will conduct an interview to initiate the recruitment process. This process begins with the recruiter determining if you meet the basic qualification requirements. Expect a review of your education level, financial record, background investigation, interests, criminal record or drug history, height and weight, age, and citizenship. Once basic qualifications have been established, the recruiter refers you to an officer recruiter who will schedule you to take the AFOQT and a physical exam. After this, you will meet with your officer recruiter to discuss your AFOQT scores and any medical issue that may preclude your entrance to an officer commissioning school leading to an appointment as an officer. During this meeting, the officer recruiter will discuss which branch(es) of service you qualify for and possible career options for you to choose from. Your recruiter can respond to any concerns or questions you have along the way.

PRACTICE TEST ONE

VERBAL ANALOGIES

This part of the test measures your ability to reason and see relationships among words. You are to choose the option that best completes the analogy developed at the beginning of each statement.

1. TIDY is to FASTIDIOUS as MESSY is to
    (A) ORGANIZED
    (B) MALICIOUS
    (C) SILENT
    (D) NEAT
    (E) CHAOTIC

2. JARGON is to TERMINOLOGY as NONCHALANCE is to
    (A) CONCERN
    (B) FEAR
    (C) CASUALNESS
    (D) JOY
    (E) IRRITATION

3. 100 is to 20 as
    (A) 1,000 is to 10
    (B) 1 is to 0.5
    (C) 5 is to 15
    (D) DOLLAR is to PENNY
    (E) 10 is to 2

4. GENEROSITY is to GRATITUDE as
    (A) SYMPATHY is to COMPASSION
    (B) DERISION is to HUMILIATION
    (C) NEGLIGENCE is to CAUTIOUSNESS
    (D) THOUGHTFULNESS is to CONSIDERATION
    (E) MALICE is to CRUELTY

5. FACILITATE is to ASSIST as OBLITERATE is to
    (A) CONSTRUCT
    (B) CREATE
    (C) QUESTION
    (D) BOTHER
    (E) DESTROY

6. DECADE is to 10 as
    (A) FINGERS are to 10
    (B) 50 is to 500
    (C) 13 is to 26
    (D) CENTURY is to 100
    (E) FIFTY is to 50

7. ANTELOPE is to HERD as LION is to
- **(A)** PRIDE
- **(B)** TROOP
- **(C)** FLOCK
- **(D)** ZEBRA
- **(E)** PACK

8. MARRED is to REPAIRED as EFFACED is to
- **(A)** OBLITERATED
- **(B)** HIGHLIGHTED
- **(C)** STEADIED
- **(D)** BACKED
- **(E)** DISRESPECTED

9. IRRITATED is to FURIOUS as
- **(A)** SATISFIED is to CONTENTED
- **(B)** GLAD is to JUBILANT
- **(C)** UNHAPPY is to DISPLEASED
- **(D)** HOPELESS is to OPTIMISTIC
- **(E)** CALM is to TRANQUIL

10. CAREFUL is to PAINSTAKING as GOOD is to
- **(A)** OUTSTANDING
- **(B)** DECENT
- **(C)** PASSABLE
- **(D)** CRUEL
- **(E)** UNSATISFACTORY

11. OBSCURE is to HIDDEN as MALICIOUS is to
- **(A)** WICKED
- **(B)** LONELY
- **(C)** SHY
- **(D)** KIND
- **(E)** GREEDY

12. DIMINUTIVE is to COLOSSAL as PENNILESS is to
- **(A)** PETITE
- **(B)** DOLLARS
- **(C)** AFFLUENT
- **(D)** BROKE
- **(E)** CURRENCY

13. MASON is to BRICKS as CARPENTER is to
- **(A)** CONSTRUCTION
- **(B)** HAMMERS
- **(C)** STRUCTURES
- **(D)** WOOD
- **(E)** MEASURES

14. DOWNPOUR is to FLOODING as
- **(A)** EARTHQUAKE is to DESTRUCTION
- **(B)** DROUGHT is to ABUNDANCE
- **(C)** TORNADO is to HURRICANE
- **(D)** EXPLOSION is to BLAST
- **(E)** SOIL is to MUDDY

15. PEDAL is to BICYCLE as ZIPPER is to
- **(A)** CLOSURE
- **(B)** METAL
- **(C)** BUTTON
- **(D)** INVENTION
- **(E)** JACKET

16. 5 is to 5,000 as
- **(A)** 10 is to 100
- **(B)** 20 is to 20,000
- **(C)** 30 is to 90
- **(D)** 40 is to 45
- **(E)** 50 is to 501

17. STUDENT is to CLASS as TEACHER is to
    (A) KINDERGARTEN
    (B) INSTRUCTOR
    (C) FACULTY
    (D) CLASSROOM
    (E) PRINCIPAL

18. ODD is to BIZARRE as SILLY is to
    (A) VIVACIOUS
    (B) COMPOSED
    (C) RIDICULOUS
    (D) INCOMPREHENSIBLE
    (E) EDGY

19. CALORIES are to ENERGY as LITERS are to
    (A) CONTAINERS
    (B) LENGTH
    (C) VOLUME
    (D) HEIGHT
    (E) MILILITERS

20. ERG is to WORK as DECIBEL is to
    (A) VOLUME
    (B) WIDTH
    (C) DISTANCE
    (D) WEIGHT
    (E) SOUND

21. ELEPHANT is to LUMBERS as HUMMINGBIRD is to
    (A) FLITS
    (B) SLINKS
    (C) TROTS
    (D) CLUMPS
    (E) SQUIRMS

22. HUNGRY is to RAVENOUS as SAD is to
    (A) EMOTION
    (B) ECSTATIC
    (C) UNCONCERNED
    (D) VORACIOUS
    (E) MISERABLE

23. BORING is to MIND-NUMBING as
    (A) CURIOUS is to INDIFFERENT
    (B) OBEDIENT is to REBELLIOUS
    (C) FAMISHED is to STARVING
    (D) PARSIMONIOUS is to MISERLY
    (E) DISPLEASED is to LIVID

24. SNAKE is to SLITHERS as KANGAROO is to
    (A) AMPHIBIANS
    (B) BOUNDS
    (C) MARSUPIALS
    (D) POUCHES
    (E) SCALES

25. BEQUEATH is to INHERIT as DONATE is to
    (A) PROVIDE
    (B) RENEW
    (C) LINGER
    (D) REQUIRE
    (E) RECEIVE

ARITHMETIC REASONING

This part of the test measures your ability to use arithmetic to solve problems. Each problem is followed by five possible answers. You are to decide which one of the five choices is correct.

1. A high school cross country team sent 25 percent of its runners to a regional competition. Of these, 10 percent won medals. If 2 runners earned medals, how many members does the cross country team have?

   (A) 8
   (B) 10
   (C) 80
   (D) 125
   (E) 1250

2. Convert 55 meters to feet (round to the nearest tenth of a foot).

   (A) 16.8 feet
   (B) 21.7 feet
   (C) 139.7 feet
   (D) 165.0 feet
   (E) 180.4 feet

3. If a person reads 40 pages in 45 minutes, approximately how many minutes will it take her to read 265 pages?

   (A) 202
   (B) 236
   (C) 265
   (D) 298
   (E) 300

4. If three burgers and two orders of fries costs $26.50 and a burger costs $6.50, how much does one order of fries cost?

   (A) $1.75
   (B) $3.50
   (C) $6.75
   (D) $7.00
   (E) $10.00

5. A worker was paid $15,036 for 7 months of work. If he received the same amount each month, how much was he paid for the first 2 months?

   (A) $2,148
   (B) $4,296
   (C) $5,137
   (D) $6,444
   (E) $8,592

6. The average speed of cars on a highway (s) is inversely proportional to the number of cars on the road (n). If a car drives at 65 mph when there are 250 cars on the road, how fast will a car drive when there are 325 cars on the road?

   (A) 50 mph
   (B) 55 mph
   (C) 60 mph
   (D) 85 mph
   (E) 87 mph

7. The probability of drawing a blue marble from a bag of marbles is $\frac{1}{20}$ and the probability of drawing a red marble from the same bag is $\frac{7}{20}$ What is the probability of drawing a blue marble or a red marble?

   (A) $\frac{1}{10}$
   (B) $\frac{3}{10}$
   (C) $\frac{7}{20}$
   (D) $\frac{2}{5}$
   (E) $\frac{1}{2}$

8. The population of a town was 7,250 in 2014 and 7,375 in 2015. What was the percent increase from 2014 to 2015 to the nearest tenth of a percent?

(A) 1.5%

(B) 1.6%

(C) 1.7%

(D) 1.8%

(E) 2.0%

9. Lynn has 4 test scores in science class. Each test is worth 100 points, and Lynn has an 85% average. If Lynn scored 100% on each of the first 3 tests, what did she score on her 4th test?

(A) 40%

(B) 55%

(C) 60%

(D) 85%

(E) 100%

10. Allison used $2\frac{1}{2}$ cups of flour to make a cake, and $\frac{3}{4}$ of a cup of flour to make a pie. If she started with 4 cups of flour, how many cups of flour does she have left?

(A) $\frac{3}{4}$

(B) 1

(C) $\frac{5}{4}$

(D) $\frac{5}{2}$

(E) $\frac{13}{4}$

11. Alex cleans houses and charges $25 per bedroom, $35 per bathroom, and $40 per kitchen. If he cleans a house with 4 bedrooms, 2 bathrooms, and 1 kitchen, how much will he be paid?

(A) $205

(B) $210

(C) $215

(D) $230

(E) $245

12. Juan plans to spend 25% of his workday writing a report. If he is at work for 9 hours, how many hours will he spend writing the report?

(A) 2.25

(B) 2.50

(C) 2.75

(D) 3.25

(E) 4.00

13. Valerie receives a base salary of $740 a week for working 40 hours. For every extra hour she works, she is paid at a rate of $27.75 per hour. If Valerie works t hours in a week, which of the following equations represents the amount of money, A, she will receive?

(A) $A = 740 + 27.75(t - 40)$

(B) $A = 740 + 27.75(40 - t)$

(C) $A = 740 - 27.75(40 - t)$

(D) $A = 27.75t - 740$

(E) $A = 27.75t + 740$

14. If $\triangle ABD \sim \triangle DEF$ and the similarity ratio is 3:4, what is the measure of DE if $AB = 12$?

(A) 6

(B) 9

(C) 12

(D) 16

(E) 96

15. Justin has a summer lawn care business and earns $40 for each lawn he mows. He also pays $35 per week in business expenses. Which of the following expressions represents Justin's profit after x weeks if he mows m number of lawns?

(A) $40m - 35x$

(B) $40m + 35x$

(C) $35x(40 + m)$

(D) $35(40m + x)$

(E) $40x(35 + m)$

16. Micah has invited 23 friends to his house and is having pizza for dinner. If each pizza feeds 4 people, how many pizzas should he order?

    (A) 4
    (B) 5
    (C) 6
    (D) 7
    (E) 8

17. In the fall, 425 students pass the math benchmark. In the spring, 680 students pass the same benchmark. What is the percentage increase in passing scores from fall to spring?

    (A) 37.5%
    (B) 55%
    (C) 60%
    (D) 62.5%
    (E) 80%

18. Maria paid $24.65 for her meal at a restaurant. If that price included a tax of 8.25 percent, what was the price of the meal before tax?

    (A) $22.61
    (B) $22.68
    (C) $22.77
    (D) $22.82
    (E) $22.93

19. A high school football team played 12 games in a season. If they won 75 percent of their games, how many games did they lose?

    (A) 3
    (B) 4
    (C) 6
    (D) 9
    (E) 10

20. Aprille has $50 to buy the items on her shopping list. Assuming there is no sales tax, about how much change will Aprille receive after buying all the items on her list?

Aprille's List

ITEM	PRICE
Hammer	$13.24
Screwdriver	$11.99
Nails	$4.27
Wrench	$5.60

    (A) $12
    (B) $13
    (C) $14
    (D) $15
    (E) $16

21. A fruit stand sells apples, bananas, and oranges at a ratio of 3:2:1. If the fruit stand sells 20 bananas, how many total pieces of fruit does the fruit stand sell?

    (A) 10
    (B) 30
    (C) 40
    (D) 50
    (E) 60

22. A company interviewed 21 applicants for a recent opening. Of these applicants, 7 wore blue and 6 wore white, while 5 applicants wore both blue and white. What is the number of applicants who wore neither blue nor white?

    (A) 1
    (B) 6
    (C) 8
    (D) 12
    (E) 13

23. In the sequence below, each term is found by finding the difference between the previous two numbers and mulitplying the result by −3. What is the 6th term of the sequence?

{3, 0, −9, −36, ... }

(A) −81

(B) −135

(C) 45

(D) 81

(E) 135

24. If the length of a rectangle is increased by 40% and its width is decreased by 40%, what is the effect on the rectangle's area?

(A) The area is the same.

(B) It increases by 16%.

(C) It increases by 20%.

(D) It decreases by 16%.

(E) It decreases by 20%.

25. If a plane travels 2775 miles in 3 hours, how far will it travel in 5 hours?

(A) 1665 miles

(B) 3475 miles

(C) 4625 miles

(D) 5550 miles

(E) 13,875 miles

WORD KNOWLEDGE

This part of the test measures your knowledge of words and their meanings. For each question, you are to choose the word below that is closest in meaning to the capitalized word above.

1. PACIFY
   (A) soothe
   (B) transport
   (C) bathe
   (D) motivate
   (E) nurture

2. INDOLENCE
   (A) serenity
   (B) bliss
   (C) laziness
   (D) tolerance
   (E) sympathy

3. ARDENT
   (A) silvery
   (B) stubborn
   (C) metallic
   (D) passionate
   (E) vicious

4. COUNTENANCE
   (A) strict law
   (B) total amount
   (C) fancy clothing
   (D) body language
   (E) facial expression

5. CHARISMA
   (A) love
   (B) motion
   (C) character
   (D) sneakiness
   (E) attractiveness

6. DAUNT
   (A) thrill
   (B) shove
   (C) intimidate
   (D) encourage
   (E) silence

7. CREDULOUS
   (A) naïve
   (B) amazing
   (C) tedious
   (D) optimistic
   (E) genuine

8. LABYRINTH
   (A) maze
   (B) dungeon
   (C) workshop
   (D) basement
   (E) laboratory

9. SACROSANCT
   (A) handy
   (B) quiet
   (C) dim
   (D) secure
   (E) holy

10. RUDIMENTARY
    (A) impolite
    (B) basic
    (C) juvenile
    (D) innovative
    (E) additional

11. IMPARTIAL
   (A) fond
   (B) incomplete
   (C) objective
   (D) mathematical
   (E) heartless

12. REITERATE
   (A) recite
   (B) repeat
   (C) reunite
   (D) reread
   (E) return

13. PRECEDENT
   (A) event
   (B) birth
   (C) idea
   (D) model
   (E) leader

14. PRUDENT
   (A) sensible
   (B) inquisitive
   (C) terrified
   (D) squeamish
   (E) modest

15. FIGURATIVE
   (A) lofty
   (B) lengthy
   (C) nonliteral
   (D) uncooperative
   (E) hypocritical

16. INNOCUOUS
   (A) susceptible
   (B) sickly
   (C) bland
   (D) cautious
   (E) senseless

17. NEGLIGENCE
   (A) malice
   (B) immorality
   (C) inattention
   (D) nothingness
   (E) magnetism

18. LAX
   (A) salty
   (B) decorative
   (C) malicious
   (D) meddlesome
   (E) permissive

19. EQUIVOCATE
   (A) be evasive
   (B) be dishonest
   (C) devise plots
   (D) trap others
   (E) add numbers

20. PONDEROUS
   (A) thoughtful
   (B) marshy
   (C) boisterous
   (D) rotting
   (E) weighty

21. CIRCUMSPECT
   (A) round
   (B) viewed
   (C) guarded
   (D) dominant
   (E) winding

22. ASSIDUOUS
   (A) complicated
   (B) critical
   (C) generous
   (D) bitter
   (E) industrious

23. SOLICITOUS
    (A) attentive
    (B) persuasive
    (C) cheerful
    (D) serene
    (E) fiery

24. APTITUDE
    (A) talent for socializing
    (B) constant hunger
    (C) capacity to learn
    (D) love of pleasure
    (E) lofty height

25. JEOPARDY
    (A) prediction
    (B) danger
    (C) choice
    (D) destiny
    (E) nature

MATH KNOWLEDGE

This part of the test measures your knowledge of mathematical terms and principles. Each problem is followed by five possible answers. You are to decide which one of the five choices is correct.

1. Which of the following is equivalent to $z^3(z + 2)^2 - 4z^3 + 2$?

   (A) 2
   (B) $z^5 + 4z^4 + 4z^3 + 2$
   (C) $z^6 + 4z^3 + 2$
   (D) $z^5 + 4z^4 + 2$
   (E) $z^5 + 4z^3 + 6$

2. Simplify: $\frac{(3x^2y^2)^2}{3^3x^{-2}y^3}$

   (A) $3x^6y$
   (B) $\frac{x^6y}{3}$
   (C) $\frac{x^4}{3y}$
   (D) $\frac{3x^4}{y}$
   (E) $\frac{x^6y}{3}$

3. What is the value of $\left(\frac{1}{2}\right)^3$?

   (A) $\frac{1}{8}$
   (B) $\frac{1}{6}$
   (C) $\frac{1}{4}$
   (D) $\frac{3}{8}$
   (E) $\frac{3}{2}$

4. How many cubic feet of soil would be required to cover a circular garden with a diameter of 8 feet if the soil needs to be 0.5 feet deep (use $\pi = 3.14$)?

   (A) 6.28 ft^3
   (B) 12.56 ft^3
   (C) 25.12 ft^3
   (D) 100.48 ft^3
   (E) 200.96 ft^3

5. Which of the following sets of shapes are NOT all similar to each other?

   (A) right triangles
   (B) spheres
   (C) 30–60–90 triangles
   (D) squares
   (E) cubes

6. The line of best fit is calculated for a data set that tracks the number of miles that passenger cars traveled annually in the US from 1960 to 2010. In the model, $x = 0$ represents the year 1960, and y is the number of miles traveled in billions. If the line of best fit is $y = 0.0293x + 0.563$, approximately how many additional miles were traveled for every 5 years that passed?

   (A) 0.0293 billion
   (B) 0.1465 billion
   (C) 0.5630 billion
   (D) 0.7100 billion
   (E) 2.9615 billion

7. Simplify: $\sqrt[3]{64} + \sqrt[3]{729}$

   (A) 13
   (B) 15
   (C) 17
   (D) 31
   (E) 35

8. What is the remainder when 397 is divided by 4?

   (A) 0
   (B) 1
   (C) 2
   (D) 3
   (E) 4

9. If the surface area of a cylinder with radius of 4 feet is 48π square feet, what is its volume?

(A) 1π ft.^{3}

(B) 16π ft.^{3}

(C) 32π ft.^{3}

(D) 48π ft.^{3}

(E) 64π ft.^{3}

10. Which expression is equivalent to $(x + 3)(x - 2)(x + 4)$?

(A) $x^3 - 2x + 24$

(B) $x^3 + 5x - 24$

(C) $x^3 + 9x^2 - 24$

(D) $x^3 + 5x^2 - 2x - 24$

(E) $x^3 + 9x^2 + 6x + 24$

11. Which of the following is a solution of the given equation?

$4(m + 4)^2 - 4m^2 + 20 = 276$

(A) 3

(B) 4

(C) 6

(D) 12

(E) 24

12. What is the x-intercept of the given equation?

$10x + 10y = 10$

(A) $(1, 0)$

(B) $(0, 1)$

(C) $(0, 0)$

(D) $(1, 1)$

(E) $(10, 10)$

13. Which of the following is closest in value to $129{,}113 + 34{,}602$?

(A) 162,000

B) 163,000

(C) 164,000

(D) 165,000

(E) 166,000

14. Solve for x: $x^2 - 3x - 18 = 0$

(A) $x = -3$

(B) $x = 2$

(C) $x = -3$ and $x = 6$

(D) $x = 2$ and $x = 3$

(E) $x = 3$ and $x = -6$

15. The coordinates of point A are $(7, 12)$ and the coordinates of point C are $(-3, 10)$. If C is the midpoint of $\overline{AB}$, what are the coordinates of point B?

(A) $(-13, 8)$

(B) $(-13, 11)$

(C) $(2, 11)$

(D) $(2, 14)$

(E) $(17, 14)$

16. Which of the following could be the perimeter of a triangle with two sides that measure 13 and 5?

(A) 24.5

(B) 26.5

(C) 36

(D) 37

(E) 37.5

17. What is $\frac{5}{8}$ as a percent?

(A) 1.6%

(B) 16%

(C) 0.625%

(D) 6.25%

(E) 62.5%

18. What is the value of z in the following system?

$z - 2x = 14$

$2z - 6x = 18$

(A) -7

(B) -2

(C) 3

(D) 5

(E) 24

19. What is the value of the expression $15m + 2n^2 - 7$ if $m = 3$ and $n = -4$?

(A) -49

(B) -31

(C) 6

(D) 70

(E) 102

20. Which number has the greatest value?

(A) 9299 ones

(B) 903 tens

(C) 93 hundreds

(D) 9 thousands

(E) 9 thousandths

21. Which of the following is an equation of the line that passes through the points $(4, -3)$ and $(-2, 9)$ in the xy-plane?

(A) $y = -2x + 5$

(B) $y = -\frac{1}{2}x - 1$

(C) $y = \frac{1}{2}x - 5$

(D) $y = 2x - 11$

(E) $y = 4x + 1$

22. W, X, Y, and Z lie on a circle with center A. If the diameter of the circle is 75, what is the sum of $\overline{AW}$, $\overline{AX}$, $\overline{AY}$, and $\overline{AZ}$?

(A) 75

(B) 100

(C) 125

(D) 300

(E) 150

23. Which inequality is equivalent to $10 \le k - 5$?

(A) $k \le 15$

(B) $k \ge 15$

(C) $k \le 5$

(D) $k \ge 5$

(E) $k \le 10$

24. Rectangular water tank A is 5 feet long, 10 feet wide, and 4 feet tall. Rectangular tank B is 5 feet long, 5 feet wide, and 4 feet tall. If the same amount of water is poured into both tanks and the height of the water in Tank A is 1 foot, how high will the water be in Tank B?

(A) 1 foot

(B) 2 feet

(C) 3 feet

(D) 4 feet

(E) 5 feet

25. The inequality $2a - 5b > 12$ is true for which values of a and b?

(A) $a = 2$ and $b = 6$

(B) $a = 1$ and $b = -3$

(C) $a = -1$ and $b = 3$

(D) $a = 7$ and $b = 2$

(E) $a = 2$ and $b = -1$

READING COMPREHENSION

This part of the test measures your ability to read and understand written material. Each passage is followed by a series of multiple-choice questions. You are to choose the option that best answers the question based on the passage. No additional information or specific knowledge is needed.

Much of the complexity of the Korean War derives from the very different perspectives of the participants. In reality, the conflict was actually three wars in one, with each faction believing itself to be protecting Korea from an oppressive, invasive force. The participants can be visualized as three concentric circles of increasingly indirect interest in the war.

In the outermost circle were the United States and the Soviet Union. For these two countries, Korea was simply the next stage in their ongoing battle for global power. In 1945, the Soviets invaded Manchuria in their campaign against Japan and seized control of Korea. When the war ended, the United States—in agreement with the Soviet Union—sent an expeditionary force to southern Korea to disarm and repatriate the hundreds of thousands of Japanese soldiers and citizens there. With Soviet troops in the north and American troops in the south, neither side wanted to relinquish control. The Soviets, excluded from the occupation of Japan, feared an American attempt to control Asia; the United States feared the same from the Soviets as the USSR became increasingly supportive of the Chinese communists.

As a compromise, the two powers decided to temporarily divide Korea on the thirty-eighth parallel, keeping their respective troops in place. Each installed a pliable government, but tensions grew within each part of Korea. Internal resistance to foreign occupation as well as aggressive moves from the north and the Soviet Union to reunite the country ultimately resulted in war in 1950.

In the middle ring of participants were the nations of Asia. Suffering from the aftermath of World War II, few Asian countries were able to actively participate in the Korean War, although all watched events closely. The exception was China, which was undergoing its own political transformation.

With the support of the Soviet Union, Mao Zedong seized control of China and established the People's Republic of China in 1949. The United States perceived Zedong's success to be a serious blow to both American political ideas and American global power. But Zedong's dominance was not complete: a second Chinese government persisted, exiled to Taiwan but politically sanctioned by the United States. Korea's fate, then, was dependent on the future security of each of these two Chinas. In addition, all of Asia was concerned about containing Japan, which had pursued aggressive imperialism on the mainland since the end of the nineteenth century, conquering Korea, the Philippines, Thailand, and parts of China. The question of the Korean War became a question of which government could best keep Japan at bay.

Finally, in the innermost circle were North Korea and South Korea, the two supposedly temporary states created by the World War II allies and controlled by opposing governments. For these two factions, the war was a civil war. Before 1945, Korea did not view itself as two different countries but as one unified nation. However, that nation had been occupied by Japan for much of its history, making it automatically resistant to the interference of both Soviet and American troops. The division of the country, while militarily reasonable for the United States and the Soviet Union, was incredibly damaging to Korea itself. The country's most valuable resources—its gold and coal mines, fertilizer and concrete plants, and hydroelectric power system—were all concentrated in the northern zone. However, the scarce arable land and two-thirds of the people were in the southern zone. Economically crippled and resentful of another long occupation, communist leaders in the South revolted against American troops, attempting to seize control from the UN-approved government.

Kim Il-sung, the communist leader of North Korea, enjoying enthusiastic support from the Soviet Union and reluctantly backed by China, capitalized on the unrest to attempt to reunite the country under his rule. The resulting war brought all these various actors, motivations, and agendas into a conflict in which no clear winner would emerge. The only guarantee who was a loser: the Korean nation.

1. The main idea of the passage is that
    (A) the Korean War was unwinnable because different countries viewed the conflict differently.
    (B) the Korean War involved many actors from both within and outside of Asia.
    (C) the Korean people had little involvement in the issues that ultimately resulted in the war.
    (D) the United States and the Soviet Union both feared that the other wanted to control Asia.
    (E) the division of Korea on the thirty-eighth parallel was economically devastating for the country.

2. According to the passage, why was Japan viewed as a threat?
    (A) Japan actively opposed the spread of communism throughout Asia.
    (B) Japan's rise to power weakened the influence of American ideals in Asia.
    (C) Hundreds of thousands of Japanese soldiers remained stationed in Korea and throughout Asia.
    (D) Japan had previously used its military to extend control over much of mainland Asia.
    (E) Japanese support helped to maintain the exiled Chinese government in opposition to Mao Zedong.

3. It can be inferred from the passage that in the period leading up to the Korean War,
    (A) both North and South Koreans actually wanted a communist government.
    (B) tensions between the United States and the Soviet Union increased.
    (C) Mao Zedong strongly influenced Kim Il-Sung's aggression against the south.
    (D) most Koreans resented the American occupation of Japan.
    (E) the Soviet Union greatly profited from the industrial resources in North Korea.

4. The primary purpose of the passage is to
    (A) describe the Asian perspective on the Korean War.
    (B) discuss the Korean War's impact on the United States and the Soviet Union.
    (C) provide a history of the lead-up to the Korean War.
    (D) inform the reader about the different leaders involved in the Korean War.
    (E) explain the reasons why the Korean War was so complicated.

CONTINUE

5. Which of the following is NOT a fact stated in the passage?

    (A) The Soviet Union had troops in Korea first, followed by the United States.

    (B) The majority of Korea's population was concentrated in the south of the country.

    (C) The United States and the Soviet Union agreed to permanently divide Korea into two countries.

    (D) Koreans were fed up with occupying forces and resistant to more foreign troops.

    (E) In 1949, two competing governments claimed to rule China.

6. With which of the following claims about the Korean War would the author most likely agree?

    (A) If the United States had pursued a different policy in Japan, China would not have supported North Korea.

    (B) The Soviet Union was hesitant to risk a conflict with the United States in the postwar era.

    (C) Japanese occupation left Korea unable to govern itself or to thrive economically.

    (D) The actions of the United States and the Soviet Union increased conflict in Korea and ultimately led to war.

    (E) Kim Il-sung would not have attempted an invasion of the south if he had the economic means to support his citizens.

By 1993, US troops were deeply involved in trying to end Somalia's complicated and violent civil war involving competing warlords and clans. Because of the deeply fractured nature of the country at the time, the US mission was a daunting task without a clear goal. American strategy involved deploying American Special Forces, or Army Rangers, on raids to capture key members of the various factions that were causing the most strife and conflict, with particular focus on the Somali National Alliance (SNA), a group organized under the warlord Mohamed Aidid. Due to American technological superiority, many of these raids were very successful, increasing US confidence.

In October of 1993, US forces received intelligence that some of Aidid's top officials would be gathering at a hotel in the heart of the capital city of Mogadishu, which was also deep in Aidid's territory. Military leaders planned a raid to seize the officials, thereby delivering a severe blow to the SNA. The mission, known as the Battle of Mogadishu, or—more popularly—as Black Hawk Down, did not go as planned. Rather than quickly extract their targets, the Rangers were bogged down by gunfire on the streets, and the two Black Hawk helicopters providing support were shot down, turning the mission into an unplanned search and rescue as the Rangers attempted to save the crew of the helicopters. While the mission was ultimately successful in obtaining its targets, it was a strategic failure that resulted in significant Somali and American loss of life and a swell of opposition to the overall mission in Somalia at home.

The disintegration of the mission shocked military leaders at the time and highlighted a significantly flawed approach to urban warfare. Previous American raids had been successful for three primary reasons: (1) they occurred in more remote locations, (2) they occurred under the cover of night, and (3) they utilized the element of surprise by maximizing American technological superiority. The first two factors were altered in the Battle of Mogadishu simply by circumstance: the leaders were meeting in the center of a densely populated area in the middle of the day. While that could not be avoided, neither the mission planners nor the Rangers adequately planned for these changes. The Rangers assumed the mission would be quick, like others had been, and lightened their equipment loads, leaving behind water and night-vision goggles. The mission planners did not realize that a daylight mission in the heart of Aidid's territory would be significantly more complicated, and so they did not allow sufficient flexibility for the commander, nor did they provide sufficient contingencies.

Most significantly, though, US officials overestimated the advantage their technology provided. First, American overconfidence resulted in little attempt at secrecy in planning. American forces were based out of the airport, giving many Somali contractors regular access to American plans, which were then leaked to the SNA. They were prepared for the American raid before it ever began. Also, while American helicopters provided stealth and speed, they also became the Rangers' downfall.

The SNA studied American tactical patterns and adjusted their own strategies accordingly. For example, they knew that the US would use the helicopters for air support during the raid, so Aidid stationed surface-to-air missiles. They also knew that American policy was to rescue the helicopter crew once it was downed, which gave the SNA the tactical advantage. Because of the fluid and unofficial nature of factions in Somalia, friends and foes were not clearly labeled, allowing SNA fighters to easily blend in and out of the densely packed city. The SNA had the objective of crippling US forces with little regard to collateral loss of life, whereas they knew American policy would be to minimize civilian deaths. This became increasingly difficult as plain-clothed SNA fighters made it hard to tell combatant from civilian.

When the images of the dead were broadcast back home, public outrage ultimately led to American withdrawal from Somalia altogether and to the country's descent into deeper chaos. American officials were very reluctant to commit US troops to future humanitarian missions, resulting in a reorientation of American foreign policy. Tactically, the Battle of Mogadishu awoke military officials to the deep complexities of urban warfare and led to increased focus on improving information gathering, developing ways of observing targets from a safe distance, and creating more flexible and thorough plans for urban missions. It also was a significant motivation for the development of the US military drone program. However, the true lasting message is that there is no surefire way to be successful in urban warfare, and the tools that make the United States so powerful can sometimes lead to its downfall.

7. The primary purpose of the passage is to
   (A) explain the reasons for American involvement in the Somalian civil war.
   (B) inform the reader about the role Army Rangers played in Somalia.
   (C) describe American domestic response to the Battle of Mogadishu.
   (D) analyze the mistakes made by Army Rangers during the Battle of Mogadishu.
   (E) identify military lessons learned from the Battle of Mogadishu.

8. According to the passage, why were helicopters a problem for US forces during the battle?
   (A) They were unable to determine who was a combatant and so were responsible for the majority of civilian deaths.
   (B) The SNA intentionally targeted them in order to shift the mission to a rescue mission.
   (C) They were unable to land in the densely populated section of Mogadishu.
   (D) The SNA had weapons designed specifically to target and destroy helicopters.
   (E) Their loud noise drew attention to the incoming Rangers and eliminated the element of surprise.

9.	It can be inferred from the passage that Mohamed Aidid
	(A)	primarily dominated in the rural, low-population areas of Somalia.
	(B)	had little understanding of military tactics and strategy.
	(C)	was the warlord believed to be most responsible for the violence in Somalia.
	(D)	wanted to capture and study American military technology.
	(E)	was the sole impediment to brokering a peace to end the civil war.

10.	Which of the following is NOT a fact stated in the passage?
	(A)	A degree of stability returned to Somalia shortly after the withdrawal of American troops.
	(B)	Most US raids in Somalia occurred at night rather than during daylight hours.
	(C)	The Rangers did succeed in obtaining the officials the mission targeted.
	(D)	The United States did not have a clear endgame in Somalia.
	(E)	The Rangers were pinned down by gunfire before the helicopters were brought down.

11.	With which of the following claims about urban warfare would the author most likely agree?
	(A)	Once its particular challenges are understood, urban environments are the best for American military missions.
	(B)	Looking back through history, the majority of US wars have been fought in urban settings.
	(C)	Thanks to advancements in military technology, battles fought in cities incur the fewest civilian deaths.
	(D)	Because of the unpredictability of urban missions, the US military should develop more effective strategies.
	(E)	Based on past experiences, military experts have learned that surprise and stealth missions are more successful in cities.

12.	In the third paragraph, the world *collateral* most nearly means
	(A)	additional.
	(B)	native.
	(C)	intentional.
	(D)	unimportant.
	(E)	unpopular.

Adapted from George Washington's farewell address given in 1796.

The great rule of conduct for us, in regard to foreign nations, is, in extending our commercial relations, to have with them as little political connection as possible. So far as we have already formed engagements, let them be fulfilled with perfect good faith. Here let us stop.

Europe has a set of primary interests, which to us have none, or a very remote relation. Hence she must be engaged in frequent controversies, the causes of which are essentially foreign to our concerns. Hence, therefore, it must be unwise in us to implicate ourselves, by artificial ties, in the ordinary vicissitudes of her politics, or the ordinary combinations and collisions of her friendships or enmities.

Our detached and distant situation invites and enables us to pursue a different course. If we remain one people, under an efficient government, the period is not far off, when we may defy material injury from external annoyance; when we may take such an attitude as will cause the neutrality, we may at any time resolve upon, to be scrupulously respected; when belligerent nations, under the impossibility of making acquisitions upon us, will not lightly hazard the giving us provocation; when we may choose peace or war, as our interest, guided by justice, shall counsel.

Why forego the advantages of so peculiar a situation? Why quit our own to stand upon foreign ground? Why, by interweaving our destiny with that of any part of Europe, entangle our peace and prosperity in the toils of European ambition, rivalship, interest, humor, or caprice?

It is our true policy to steer clear of permanent alliances with any portion of the foreign world; so far, I mean, as we are now at liberty to do it; for let me not be understood as capable of patronizing infidelity to existing engagements. I hold the maxim no less applicable to public than to private affairs, that honesty is always the best policy. I repeat it, therefore, let those engagements be observed in their genuine sense. But, in my opinion, it is unnecessary and would be unwise to extend them.

13. The main idea of the passage is that
   (A) America should back out of the alliances it has made with other countries.
   (B) America should increase its involvement with foreign nations.
   (C) America should attempt to intervene in European conflicts whenever international safety is a concern.
   (D) America should avoid foreign entanglements whenever it is able to do so.
   (E) America should weigh its options carefully before making decisions in the international sphere.

14. In the second paragraph, *vicissitudes* most nearly means
   (A) fluctuations
   (B) ideals
   (C) mutations
   (D) stagnation
   (E) rules

Skin coloration and markings have an important role to play in the world of snakes. Those intricate diamonds, stripes, and swirls help the animals hide from predators, but perhaps most importantly (for us humans, anyway), the markings can also indicate whether the snake is venomous. While it might seem counterintuitive for a venomous snake to stand out in bright red or blue, that fancy costume tells any nearby predator that approaching him would be a bad idea.

If you see a flashy-looking snake in the woods, though, those markings don't necessarily mean it's venomous: some snakes have found a way to ward off predators without the actual venom. The scarlet kingsnake, for example, has very similar markings to the venomous coral snake with whom it frequently shares a habitat. However, the kingsnake is actually nonvenomous; it's merely pretending to be dangerous to eat. A predatory hawk or eagle, usually hunting from high in the sky, can't tell the difference between the two species, and so the kingsnake gets passed over and lives another day.

15. The primary purpose of the passage is to
    (A) explain how the markings on a snake are related to whether it's venomous.
    (B) teach readers the difference between coral snakes and kingsnakes.
    (C) illustrate why snakes are dangerous.
    (D) demonstrate how animals survive in difficult environments.
    (E) disprove popular notions of the snake species.

16. In can be inferred from the passage that
    (A) the kingsnake is dangerous to humans.
    (B) the coral snake and the kingsnake are both hunted by the same predators.
    (C) it's safe to handle snakes in the woods because you can easily tell whether they're poisonous.
    (D) the kingsnake changes its markings when hawks or eagles are close by.
    (E) the coral snake and the kingsnake are equally dangerous to humans.

17. Which statement is NOT a detail from the passage?
    (A) Predators will avoid eating kingsnakes because their markings are similar to those on coral snakes.
    (B) Kingsnakes and coral snakes live in the same habitats.
    (C) The coral snake uses its coloration to hide from predators.
    (D) The kingsnake is not venomous.
    (E) Snakes' markings allow them to hide from predators.

18. In the first paragraph, the word *intricate* most nearly means
    (A) complex
    (B) colorful
    (C) purposeful
    (D) changeable
    (E) delicate

19. According to the passage, what is the difference between kingsnakes and coral snakes?
    (A) Both kingsnakes and coral snakes are nonvenomous, but coral snakes have colorful markings.
    (B) Both kingsnakes and coral snakes are venomous, but kingsnakes have colorful markings.
    (C) Kingsnakes are nonvenomous while coral snakes are venomous.
    (D) Coral snakes are nonvenomous while kingsnakes are venomous.
    (E) Coral snakes and kingsnakes have differently colored markings.

Hand washing is one of our simplest and most powerful weapons against infection. The idea behind hand washing is deceptively simple. Many illnesses are spread when people touch infected surfaces, such as door handles or other people's hands, and then touch their own eyes, mouths, or noses. So, if pathogens can be removed from the hands before they spread, infections can be prevented. When done correctly, hand washing can prevent the spread of many dangerous bacteria and viruses, including those that cause the flu, the common cold, diarrhea, and many acute respiratory illnesses.

The most basic method of hand washing involves only soap and water. Just twenty seconds of scrubbing with soap and a complete rinsing with water is enough to kill and/or wash away many pathogens. The process doesn't even require warm water—studies have shown that cold water is just as effective at reducing the number of microbes on the hands. Antibacterial soaps are also available, although several studies have shown that simple soap and cold water are just as effective.

In recent years, hand sanitizers have become popular as an alternative to hand washing. These gels, liquids, and foams contain a high concentration of alcohol (usually at least 60 percent) that kills most bacteria and fungi; they can also be effective against some, but not all, viruses. There is a downside to hand sanitizer, however. Because the sanitizer isn't rinsed from hands, it only kills pathogens and does nothing to remove organic matter. So, hands "cleaned" with hand sanitizer may still harbor pathogens. Thus, while hand sanitizer can be helpful in situations where soap and clean water aren't available, a simple hand washing is still the best option.

20. In the third paragraph, the word *harbor* most nearly means
    (A) to disguise
    (B) to hide
    (C) to wash away
    (D) to give a home
    (E) to breed

21. Which of the following is NOT a fact stated in the passage?
    (A) Many infections occur because people get pathogens on their hands and then touch their own eyes, mouths, or noses.
    (B) Antibacterial soaps and warm water are the best way to remove pathogens from hands.
    (C) Most hand sanitizers have a concentration of at least 60 percent alcohol.
    (D) Hand sanitizer can be an acceptable alternative to hand washing when soap and water aren't available.
    (E) While hand sanitizer kills most bacteria, it does nothing to remove them from the users' hands.

22. Knowing that the temperature of the water does not affect the efficacy of hand washing, it can be inferred from the passage that water plays an important role in hand washing because it
    (A) has antibacterial properties.
    (B) physically removes pathogens from hands.
    (C) cools hands to make them inhospitable to dangerous bacteria.
    (D) is hot enough to kill bacteria.
    (E) hydrates the skin.

23. Which of the following is the best summary of this passage?

(A) Many diseases are spread by pathogens that can live on the hands. Hand washing is the best way to remove these pathogens and prevent disease.

(B) Simple hand washing can prevent the spread of many common illnesses, including the flu, the common cold, diarrhea, and many acute respiratory illnesses. Hand sanitizer can also kill the pathogens that cause these diseases.

(C) Simple hand washing with soap and cold water is an effective way to reduce the spread of disease. Antibacterial soaps and hand sanitizers may also be used but are not significantly more effective.

(D) Using hand sanitizer will kill many pathogens but will not remove organic matter. Hand washing with soap and water is a better option when available.

(E) Many people become pick up infectious diseases during their regular interactions with other people and the world around them.

24. The primary purpose of the passage is to

(A) persuade readers of the importance and effectiveness of hand washing with soap and cold water.

(B) dissuade readers from using hand sanitizer.

(C) explain how many common diseases are spread through daily interaction.

(D) describe the many ways hand washing and hand sanitizer provide health benefits.

(E) encourage readers to save money by not purchasing antibacterial soaps.

25. It can be inferred from the passage that

(A) hand washing would do little to limit infections that spread through particles in the air.

(B) hand washing is not necessary for people who do not touch their eyes, mouths, or noses with their hands.

(C) hand sanitizer serves no purpose and should not be used as an alternative to hand washing.

(D) hand sanitizer will likely soon replace hand washing as the preferred method of removing pathogens from hands.

(E) hand washing is unnecessary unless one is ill.

PHYSICAL SCIENCE

This part of the test measures your knowledge in the area of science. Each of the questions or incomplete statements is followed by five choices. You are to decide which one of the choices best answers the question or completes the statement.

1. The rate at which velocity changes is
   (A) power.
   (B) force.
   (C) displacement.
   (D) acceleration.
   (E) energy.

2. The magnitude of an earthquake refers to its
   (A) power.
   (B) energy release.
   (C) destructive ability.
   (D) depth.
   (E) location.

3. When Earth moves between the moon and the sun, it is called a(n)
   (A) solar eclipse.
   (B) lunar eclipse.
   (C) black hole.
   (D) supernova.
   (E) aurora.

4. $2C_6H_{14} + 19O_2 \rightarrow 12CO_2 + 14H_2O$
   What type of reaction is shown above?
   (A) substitution reaction
   (B) acid-base reaction
   (C) decomposition reaction
   (D) combustion reaction
   (E) synthesis reaction

5. Friction is defined as a force that always
   (A) opposes motion.
   (B) pushes down onto a surface.
   (C) rotates an object.
   (D) increases the force of gravity.
   (E) opposes the normal force.

6. A microscope makes use of which property of waves to make objects appear larger?
   (A) wavelength
   (B) diffraction
   (C) amplitude
   (D) reflection
   (E) refraction

7. Isotopes of an element will have the same number of _____ and different numbers of _____.
   (A) electrons; neutrons
   (B) neutrons; electrons
   (C) protons; neutrons
   (D) protons; electrons
   (E) electrons; protons

8. A box sliding down a ramp experiences all of the following forces EXCEPT
   (A) tension.
   (B) friction.
   (C) gravitational.
   (D) normal.
   (E) buoyant.

9. Which layer of the earth, primarily made up of iron and nickel, is composed of a very hot liquid that flows around the center?

(A) lithosphere

(B) asthenosphere

(C) mesosphere

(D) inner core

(E) outer core

10. The state of matter at which particles are most loosely packed is

(A) liquid.

(B) gas.

(C) solid.

(D) plasma.

(E) crystal.

11. Which planet orbits closest to Earth?

(A) Mercury

(B) Venus

(C) Jupiter

(D) Saturn

(E) Neptune

12. An atom has 5 electrons and 12 protons. What is the total charge of the atom?

(A) $-17e$

(B) $-7e$

(C) $+7e$

(D) $+17e$

(E) The atom is neutral.

13. Which is NOT a characteristic of a mineral?

(A) They are naturally occurring.

(B) They are organic.

(C) They are solids.

(D) They have a crystalline structure.

(E) They have a single chemical compound.

14. Which of the following describes a physical change?

(A) Water becomes ice.

(B) Batter is baked into a cake.

(C) An iron fence rusts.

(D) A firecracker explodes.

(E) Neutralizing an acid with a base.

15. Which layer of the atmosphere absorbs harmful ultraviolet radiation from the sun?

(A) the mesosphere

(B) the stratosphere

(C) the troposphere

(D) the thermosphere

(E) the exosphere

16. Which statement about the solar system is true?

(A) Earth is much closer to the sun than it is to other stars.

(B) The moon is closer to Venus than it is to Earth.

(C) At certain times of the year, Jupiter is closer to the sun than Earth is.

(D) Mercury is the closest planet to Earth.

(E) Uranus is closer to the sun than Jupiter.

17. Which trait defines a saturated solution?

(A) The solute and solvent are not chemically bonded.

(B) Both the solute and solvent are liquid.

(C) The solute is distributed evenly throughout the solution.

(D) The solute is unevenly distributed throughout the solution.

(E) No more solute can be dissolved in the solution.

18. Which of the following is caused by geothermal heat?
    (A) geysers
    (B) glaciers
    (C) tsunamis
    (D) tornadoes
    (E) hurricanes

19. Energy is stored in a compressed spring in the form of
    (A) chemical potential energy.
    (B) elastic potential energy.
    (C) gravitational potential energy.
    (D) electric potential energy.
    (E) kinetic energy.

20. How long does it take the earth to rotate on its axis?
    (A) one hour
    (B) one day
    (C) one month
    (D) one year
    (E) one century

TABLE READING

This part of the test measures your ability to read a table quickly and accurately. Your task will be to find the block where the column and row intersect, note the number that appears there, and then find this number among the five answer options.

		x-value					
		1,000	**1,200**	**1,300**	**1,500**	**1,750**	**1,800**
	65	0.42	0.51	0.55	0.64	0.74	0.76
	70	0.46	0.55	0.59	0.69	0.80	0.82
y-value	**72**	0.47	0.56	0.61	0.71	0.82	0.85
	75	0.49	0.59	0.64	0.74	0.86	0.88
	78	0.51	0.61	0.66	0.76	0.89	0.92

	x	y	(A)	(B)	(C)	(D)	(E)
1.	1,300	72	0.61	0.59	0.71	0.64	0.55
2.	1,500	75	0.69	0.64	0.71	0.74	0.86
3.	1,800	65	0.82	0.76	0.74	0.80	0.92
4.	1,200	78	0.51	0.66	0.61	0.59	0.56
5.	1,750	70	0.86	0.82	0.74	0.69	0.80

Comparison of Measurements

LITERS	US CUPS	IMPERIAL CUPS
1.5	6.25	5.28
2	8.33	7.04
2.5	10.42	8.80
3	12.50	10.56
3.5	14.58	12.32
4	16.67	14.08
4.5	18.75	15.84
5	20.83	17.60

6. How many US cups equal 4 liters?
   - **(A)** 12.50
   - **(B)** 10.42
   - **(C)** 18.75
   - **(D)** 10.56
   - **(E)** 16.67

7. How many liters equal 14.08 Imperial cups?
   - **(A)** 4.5
   - **(B)** 5
   - **(C)** 2.5
   - **(D)** 4
   - **(E)** 3

8. How many Imperial cups equal 12.50 US cups?

(A) 3
(B) 10.56
(C) 12.52
(D) 14.58
(E) 20.83

9. How many liters equal 8.80 Imperial cups?

(A) 1.5
(B) 2
(C) 2.5
(D) 3.5
(E) 4

10. How many US cups equal 15.84 Imperial cups?

(A) 4
(B) 10.42
(C) 14.58
(D) 16.67
(E) 18.75

Reciprocal Runway Numbering

If the North/East End of the Runway is Numbered	then the South/West End of the Runway is Numbered	If the North/East End of the Runway is Numbered	then the South/West End of the Runway is Numbered	If the North/East End of the Runway is Numbered	then the South/West End of the Runway is Numbered
01	19	07	25	13	31
02	20	08	26	14	32
03	21	09	27	15	33
04	22	10	28	16	34
05	23	11	29	17	35
06	24	12	30	18	36

11. If the North/East end of the runway is numbered 13, what is the South/West end of that runway numbered?

(A) 17
(B) 19
(C) 28
(D) 31
(E) 33

12. If the South/West end of the runway is numbered 23, what is the North/East end of that runway numbered?

(A) 02
(B) 03
(C) 05
(D) 08
(E) 23

13. If the North/East end of the runway is numbered 11, what is the South/West end of that runway numbered?

(A) 15
(B) 20
(C) 23
(D) 25
(E) 29

15. If the North/East end of the runway is numbered 02, what is the South/West end of that runway numbered?

(A) 20
(B) 25
(C) 27
(D) 28
(E) 33

14. If the South/West end of the runway is numbered 35, what is the North/East end of that runway numbered?

(A) 15
(B) 17
(C) 20
(D) 24
(E) 35

Basic Pay of Air Force Officer

YEARS OF SERVICE

		0 – 2	3	4	5
	O-1	35,668	37,126	44,881	44,881
	O-2	41,094	46,803	53,903	55,724
RANK	O-3	47,563	53,913	58,190	63,446
	O-4	54,093	62,618	66,798	67,726
	O-5	62,694	70,628	75,513	76,435
	O-6	75,204	82,623	88,045	88,045

	Years of Service	Rank	(A)	(B)	(C)	(D)	(E)
16.	4	O-2	53,903	58,190	46,803	41,904	55,724
17.	2	O-3	54,093	41,094	63,446	47,563	53,913
18.	5	O-4	66,798	67,726	75,513	62,618	63,446
19.	0	O-2	35,668	47,563	41,094	37,126	46,803
20.	3	O-4	54,093	62,618	66,798	70,628	62,694

Speed Comparison (Statute mph converted to Knots and Nautical mph)

STATUTE MILES PER HOUR (MPH)	KNOTS (KTS)	NAUTICAL MILES PER HOUR (MPH)
6.25	5.28	5.43
70	60.8	60.83
90	78.2	78.21
115	100	99.93
138	120	119.92
172.6	150	149.99
200	173.8	173.79
350	304.14	304.14

21. If traveling at 150 kts, what does that equate to in statute mph?
   (A) 119.92
   (B) 149.99
   (C) 150
   (D) 172.6
   (E) 200

22. How many nautical mph equates to 115 statute mph?
   (A) 78.21
   (B) 99.93
   (C) 100
   (D) 120
   (E) 138

23. How many knots equate to 200 statute mph?
   (A) 60.83
   (B) 115

   (C) 173.8
   (D) 200
   (E) 304.14

24. How many knots equate to 60.83 nautical mph?
   (A) 60.8
   (B) 70
   (C) 78.2
   (D) 100
   (E) 115

25. An airplane traveling at 350 mph equates to how many knots?
   (A) 150
   (B) 172.6
   (C) 173.8
   (D) 200
   (E) 304.14

US Currency Exchange (approximate)

US ($)	EUROPEAN UNION (EUROS)	BRITISH (POUNDS)
1	0.93	0.80
150	139.55	120.31
200	186.08	160.41
300	279.14	240.62
400	372.19	320.84
500	465.23	401.05

26. How many British pounds would $400 buy?

(A) 186.08

(B) 160.41

(C) 320.84

(D) 372.19

(E) 401.05u

27. How many euros would $200 buy?

(A) 0.93

(B) 186.08

(C) 160.41

(D) 200.00

(E) 240.62

28. How many British pounds would $150 buy?

(A) 0.80

(B) 120.31

(C) 139.55

(D) 150.00

(E) 240.62

29. When converting $300 into pounds, how much would be received?

(A) 120.31

(B) 139.55

(C) 240.62

(D) 279.14

(E) 372.19

30. How many euros would $500 buy?

(A) 373.12

(B) 418.69

(C) 465.23

(D) 481.25

(E) 558.27

		x-value					
		5	**10**	**30**	**35**	**40**	**50**
	A	125	164	324	425	846	1,215
	B	274	464	512	784	623	856
y-value	**C**	613	444	754	825	1,012	873
	D	303	586	715	289	684	691
	E	124	714	386	255	784	634
	F	379	180	730	426	741	909

	_x_	_y_	(A)	(B)	(C)	(D)	(E)
31.	35	B	164	425	754	784	846
32.	5	E	124	125	379	586	634
33.	30	A	164	324	444	512	715
34.	10	C	274	303	444	464	586
35.	40	D	180	289	623	684	909

Celsius (°C) and Fahrenheit (°F) Temperature Comparison

LOCATION	TEMP (°C)	TEMP (°F)
Boston	5	41
Chicago	13	55
Florida Keys	26	78
Harvard	6	43
Los Angeles	13	56
Macon	29	84
Minneapolis	22	72
Orlando	37	98

36. What does 56 °F equate to in °C?

(A) 6°

(B) 13°

(C) 22°

(D) 29°

(E) 84°

37. When it is 84 °F in Macon, what is it in °C?

(A) 5°

(B) 6°

(C) 13°

(D) 22°

(E) 29°

38. What does 6 °C equate in °F?

(A) 43°

(B) 55°

(C) 56°

(D) 72°

(E) 78°

39. Which location is listed with a temperature of 72 °F?

(A) Harvard

(B) Los Angeles

(C) Macon

(D) Minneapolis

(E) Orlando

40. What is the difference in °C temperature listed between the Florida Keys and Chicago?

(A) 11

(B) 12

(C) 13

(D) 14

(E) 26

INSTRUMENT COMPREHENSION

This part of the test measures your ability to determine the position of an airplane in flight from reading instruments showing its compass direction heading, amount of climb or dive, and degree of bank to right or left.

Each problem consists of two dials and four airplanes in flight. Your task is to determine which one of the four airplanes is most nearly in the position indicated by the two dials. You are always looking north at the same altitude as the four airplanes. East is always to your right as you look at the page.

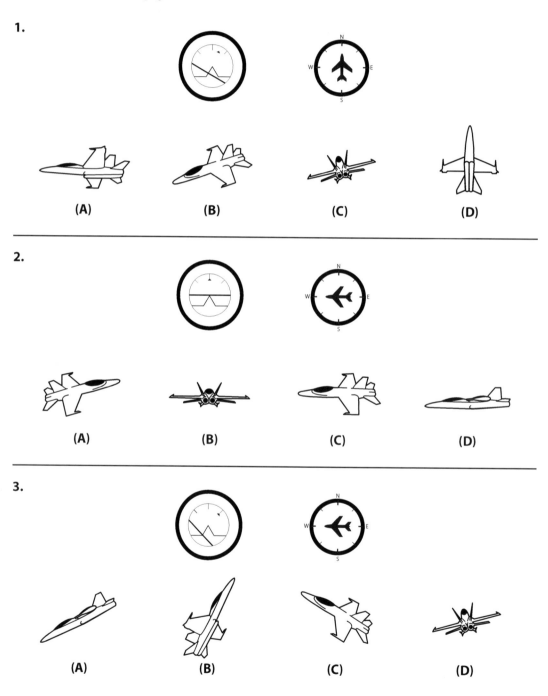

1.

(A)   (B)   (C)   (D)

2.

(A)   (B)   (C)   (D)

3.

(A)   (B)   (C)   (D)

4.

(A) (B) (C) (D)

5.

(A) (B) (C) (D)

6.

(A) (B) (C) (D)

7.

 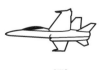

(A) (B) (C) (D)

8.

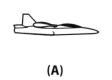

(A)

(B)

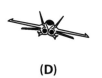

(C)

(D)

9.

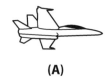

(A)

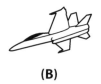

(B)

(C)

(D)

10.

(A)

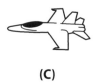

(B)

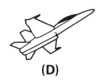

(C)

(D)

11.

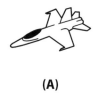

(A)

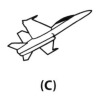

(B)

(C)

(D)

12.

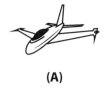

(A)　　　　　　(B)　　　　　　(C)　　　　　　(D)

13.

 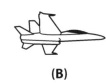 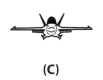

(A)　　　　　　(B)　　　　　　(C)　　　　　　(D)

14.

(A)　　　　　　(B)　　　　　　(C)　　　　　　(D)

15.

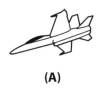  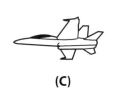

(A)　　　　　　(B)　　　　　　(C)　　　　　　(D)

16.

  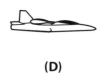

(A)　　　　　(B)　　　　　(C)　　　　　(D)

17.

  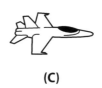 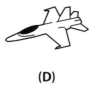

(A)　　　　　(B)　　　　　(C)　　　　　(D)

18.

 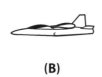 

(A)　　　　　(B)　　　　　(C)　　　　　(D)

19.

   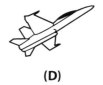

(A)　　　　　(B)　　　　　(C)　　　　　(D)

20.

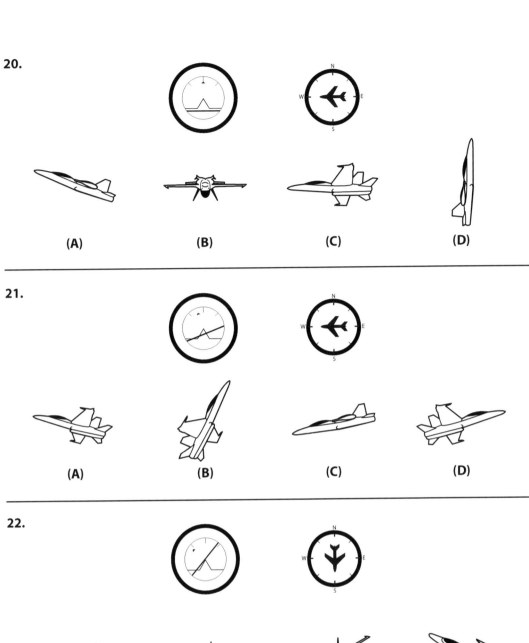

(A) (B) (C) (D)

21.

(A) (B) (C) (D)

22.

(A) (B) (C) (D)

23.

(A) (B) (C) (D)

24.

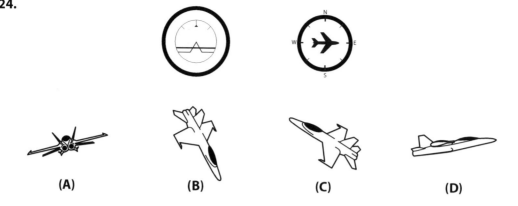

(A)   (B)   (C)   (D)

25.

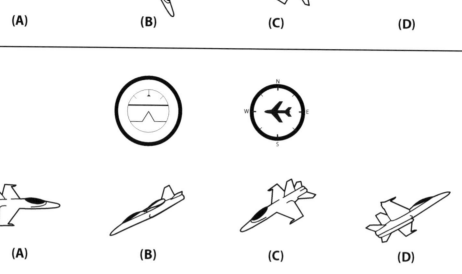

(A)   (B)   (C)   (D)

BLOCK COUNTING

Given a certain numbered block, your task is to determine how many other blocks the numbered block touches. Blocks are considered touching only if all or part of their faces touch. Blocks that only touch corners do not count. All of the blocks in each pile are the same size and shape.

Shape One

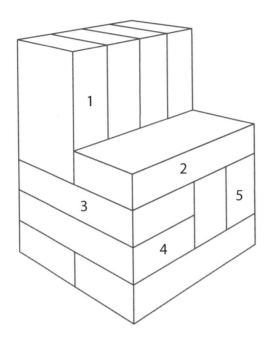

Shape Two

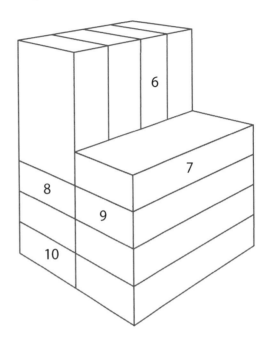

Block	A	B	C	D	E
1	5	2	7	3	1
2	3	8	7	10	9
3	5	6	4	2	1
4	3	2	4	7	1
5	6	5	9	3	7

Block	A	B	C	D	E
6	5	2	4	3	7
7	3	5	6	9	4
8	4	6	1	8	5
9	3	4	6	2	1
10	3	9	1	4	2

Shape Three

Shape Four

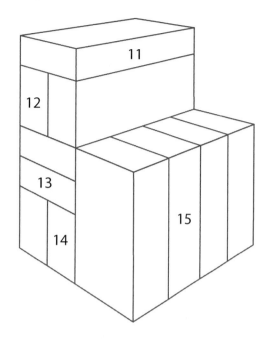

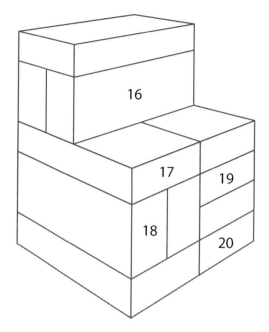

Block	A	B	C	D	E
11	4	2	1	3	9
12	5	2	7	3	4
13	7	2	6	8	9
14	7	5	6	4	8
15	5	6	2	1	7

Block	A	B	C	D	E
16	4	5	2	1	6
17	3	8	5	4	7
18	5	4	6	2	3
19	8	3	2	5	4
20	3	1	4	2	7

Shape Five

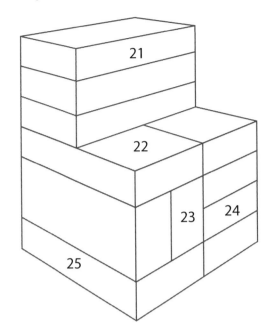

Shape Six

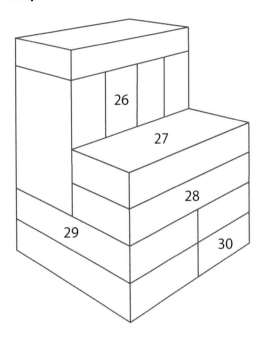

Block	A	B	C	D	E
21	2	1	7	3	4
22	4	8	3	5	9
23	7	4	5	1	2
24	6	4	2	5	3
25	1	2	4	3	5

Block	A	B	C	D	E
26	5	3	7	6	4
27	4	5	7	3	6
28	6	3	5	8	7
29	4	5	6	7	3
30	2	3	4	1	5

AVIATION INFORMATION

This part of the test measures your knowledge of aviation. Each of the questions or incomplete statements is followed by five choices. You are to decide which one of the choices best answers the question or completes the statement.

1. When raised elevators push down on the tail of an aircraft, what effect does that have on the aircraft?
   - (A) The ailerons automatically extend simultaneously.
   - (B) The nose of the aircraft lowers.
   - (C) The nose of the aircraft rises.
   - (D) The aircraft veers left.
   - (E) The aircraft veers right.

2. Which aircraft component(s) affect yaw?
   - (A) the ailerons
   - (B) the elevators
   - (C) the rudder
   - (D) the spoilers
   - (E) the wings

3. What part of a rotary-wing aircraft makes directional control possible?
   - (A) the teeter hinge
   - (B) the swashplate
   - (C) the ducted fan
   - (D) the tail boom
   - (E) the skids

4. Which type of climb produces the most altitude in a given distance?
   - (A) a best angle of climb
   - (B) a best rate of climb
   - (C) a normal climb
   - (D) a shallow climb
   - (E) a steep climb

5. If the cyclic or control wheel in a helicopter is moved forward
   - (A) the aircraft pitch changes.
   - (B) the airspeed decreases.
   - (C) the airspeed increases.
   - (D) the airspeed increases and the pitch changes.
   - (E) the aircraft tends to yaw.

6. What causes a rotary-wing aircraft to drift laterally due to tail rotor thrust?
   - (A) a coaxial rotor system
   - (B) translating tendency
   - (C) gyroscopic precession
   - (D) the tail rotor
   - (E) translational lift

7. If the airspeed indicator needle is in the yellow and approaching the red line during a maneuver, what would be the correct response?
   - (A) change attitude by 90 degrees
   - (B) decrease altitude
   - (C) decrease airspeed
   - (D) increase airspeed
   - (E) increase thrust

8. In aviation terminology, rate of climb is expressed as
   - (A) AGL
   - (B) degrees
   - (C) fpm
   - (D) knots
   - (E) MSL

9. The lateral axis of an aircraft controls which of the following?

   (A) adverse yaw
   (B) banks
   (C) pitch
   (D) roll
   (E) yaw

10. Which component allows the rotor blades to feather?

    (A) the teeter hinge
    (B) the rotor hub
    (C) the blade grips
    (D) the skids
    (E) the pitch horn

11. Which statement describes absolute altitude?

    (A) This is the altitude displayed on the altimeter.
    (B) The altitude indicator displays this altitude when the setting window reads 29.92 Hg.
    (C) This is the pressure altitude corrected for variations from standard temperature.
    (D) This is the vertical distance above MSL.
    (E) This is the vertical distance AGL.

12. Which of the following is expressed in degrees that include the area between the direction of the wind and the chord of the aircraft wing?

    (A) AOA
    (B) the artificial horizon
    (C) the lower limits of the vertical speed indicator
    (D) the pressure altitude
    (E) a stall

13. When entering and exiting Class C controlled airspace, which statement is true regarding airspace clearance?

    (A) The ATC must acknowledge the pilot by responding with the aircraft's call sign for communication to be considered established.
    (B) An ATC response of only "Standby" is enough to establish approval for entry to the controlled airspace.
    (C) No approval for clearance is needed.
    (D) Only jets flying faster than 200 mph need to request or receive approval for clearance.
    (E) A pilot does not need approval to exit Class C airspace.

14. If there is no increase in thrust, which action would result in an ultimate stall?

    (A) descending to a lower altitude
    (B) decreasing pitch
    (C) extending the ailerons and flaps
    (D) increasing pitch
    (E) turning the rudder to the left or right

15. What one of the acronyms below for all-up weight defined as the total aircraft weight at any given moment during flight?

    (A) AGW
    (B) MLW
    (C) MRW
    (D) MTOW
    (E) OEW

16. What types of turns require the pilot to input aileron pressure to return the aircraft to level flight?

(A) all turns

(B) medium and shallow turns

(C) a shallow turn

(D) medium and steep turns

(E) a trimmed turn

17. What aerodynamic principle describes the unequal lifting forces of the rotor system due to the advancing and retreating blades?

(A) weight, lift, thrust, and drag

(B) translational lift

(C) dissymmetry of lift

(D) gyroscopic precession

(E) autorotation

18. What flight control maintains the engine within optimal flight parameters?

(A) the cyclic

(B) the collective

(C) the tail rotor pedals

(D) translating tendency

(E) the throttle

19. Which statement is true about lag and trend information?

(A) Lag is the same as trend information.

(B) Lag displays real-time movement of the aircraft.

(C) Both lag and trend information display real-time movement of the aircraft.

(D) Trend information displays real-time movement of the aircraft.

(E) Trend information does not display real-time movement of the aircraft.

20. What is the unit of measure for airspeed?

(A) AOA

(B) degrees

(C) knots

(D) MSL

(E) rate of climb

ANSWER KEY

VERBAL ANALOGIES

1. **(E)**
   Someone who is *extremely* TIDY is FASTIDIOUS; a room that is *extremely* MESSY is CHAOTIC.

2. **(C)**
   JARGON is a synonym for TERMINOLOGY; NONCHALANCE is a synonym for CASUALNESS.

3. **(E)**
   100 divided by 5 equals 20; 10 divided by 5 equals 2.

4. **(B)**
   If A treats B with GENEROSITY, B is likely to feel GRATITUDE; if A treats B with DERISION, B is likely to experience HUMILIATION.

5. **(E)**
   FACILITATE is a synonym for ASSIST; OBLITERATE is a synonym for DESTROY.

6. **(D)**
   A DECADE is 10 years long; a CENTURY is 100 years long.

7. **(A)**
   An ANTELOPE is one member of a HERD; a LION is one member of a PRIDE.

8. **(B)**
   MARRED is an antonym for REPAIRED; EFFACED is an antonym for HIGHLIGHTED.

9. **(B)**
   Someone who feels *extremely* IRRITATED feels FURIOUS; someone who feels *extremely* GLAD feels JUBILANT.

10. **(A)**
    Someone who is *extremely* CAREFUL works in a PAINSTAKING manner; something that is *extremely* GOOD is OUTSTANDING.

11. **(A)**
    OBSCURE is a synonym for HIDDEN; MALICIOUS is a synonym for WICKED.

12. (C)

DIMINUTIVE is an antonym for COLOSSAL; PENNILESS is an antonym for AFFLUENT. All of these adjectives have to do with size, amount, or degree.

13. (D)

A MASON uses BRICKS to build structures; a CARPENTER uses WOOD to build them.

14. (A)

A DOWNPOUR may cause FLOODING; an EARTHQUAKE may cause DESTRUCTION.

15. (E)

A PEDAL is one part of a BICYCLE; a ZIPPER is one part of a JACKET.

16. (B)

5 times 1,000 equals 5,000; 20 times 1,000 equals 20,000.

17. (C)

A STUDENT is one member of a CLASS; a TEACHER is one member of a FACULTY.

18. (C)

Something that is *extremely* ODD is BIZARRE; something that is *extremely* SILLY is RIDICULOUS.

19. (C)

CALORIES measure ENERGY; LITERS measure liquid VOLUME.

20. (E)

An ERG is a unit of measurement that measures WORK; a DECIBEL is a unit of measurement that measures SOUND.

21. (A)

An ELEPHANT LUMBERS through the jungle; a HUMMINGBIRD FLITS through the air.

22. (E)

Someone who is *extremely* HUNGRY is RAVENOUS; someone who is *extremely* SAD is MISERABLE.

23. (E)

Something that is *extremely* BORING is MIND-NUMBING; someone who feels *extremely* DISPLEASED feels LIVID.

24. (B)

A SNAKE SLITHERS along the ground; a KANGAROO BOUNDS across the land.

25. (E)

BEQUEATH is an antonym for INHERIT; DONATE is an antonym for RECEIVE.

ARITHMETIC REASONING

1. **(C)**

   Work backwards to find the number of runners in the competition (c) and then the number of runners on the team (r).

   $\frac{2}{c} = \frac{10}{100}$

   $c = 20$

   $\frac{20}{r} = \frac{25}{100}$

   $r = 80$

2. **(E)**

   Multiply by the converstion factor to get from meters to feet.

   $55 \text{ m} \left(\frac{3.28 \text{ ft.}}{1 \text{ m}} \right) = \textbf{180.4 feet}$

3. **(D)**

   Write a proportion and then solve for x.

   $\frac{40}{45} = \frac{265}{x}$

   $40x = 11,925$

   $x = 298.125 \approx \textbf{298}$

4. **(B)**

   Find the cost of three burgers.
   Cost of 3 burgers $= 3(6.50) = 19.50$
   Subtract this value from the total costs of the meal to find the cost of the fries.

   $26.50 - 19.50 = 7$

   Divide by 2 to find the cost of one order of fries.

   $7 \div 2 = \textbf{\$3.50}$

5. **(B)**

   Write a proportion and then solve for x.

   $\frac{15,036}{7} = \frac{x}{2}$

   $7x = 30,072$

   $x = \textbf{4,296}$

6. **(A)**

   Use the formula for inversely proportional relationships to find k and then solve for s.

   $sn = k$

   $(65)(250) = k$

   $k = 16,250$

   $s(325) = 16,250$

   $s = \textbf{50}$

7. **(D)**

   Add the probability of drawing a blue marble and the probability of drawing a red marble to find the probability of drawing either a blue or red marble.

   $\frac{1}{20} + \frac{7}{20} = \frac{8}{20} = \textbf{\(\frac{2}{5}\)}$

8. **(C)**

   Use the formula for percent change.

   $percent\ change = \frac{amount\ of\ change}{original\ amount}$

   $= \frac{(7,375 - 7,250)}{7,250} = 0.017 = \textbf{1.7\%}$

9. **(A)**

   To calculate the average, add all of the scores and divide by the total number of scores. Use the variable x in place of the missing score.

   $\frac{(100 + 100 + 100 + x)}{4} = 85$

   $\frac{(300 + x)}{4} = 85$

   $(300 + x) = 340$

   $x = \textbf{40\%}$

10. **(A)**

    Add the fractions and subtract the result from the amount of flour Allison started with.

    $2\frac{1}{2} + \frac{3}{4} = \frac{5}{2} + \frac{3}{4} = \frac{10}{4} + \frac{3}{4} = \frac{13}{4}$

    $4 - \frac{13}{4} = \frac{16}{4} - \frac{13}{4} = \textbf{\(\frac{3}{4}\)}$

11. **(B)**

    Multiply the number of rooms by the cost of each room to find the total.

    $25(4) + 35(2) + 40(1) = \textbf{\$210}$

12. **(A)**

    Use the equation for percentages.

$$part = whole \times percentage =$$
$$9 \times 0.25 = \textbf{2.25}$$

13. (A)

Valerie will receive her base pay plus 27.75 for every hour she worked in addition to her 40 hours.

A = base pay + 27.75 × extra hours
$$\textbf{\textit{A} = 740 + 27.75(\textit{t} − 40)}$$

14. (D)

Set up a proportion and solve.

$$\frac{AB}{DE} = \frac{3}{4}$$
$$\frac{12}{DE} = \frac{3}{4}$$
$$3(DE) = 48$$
$$\textbf{\textit{DE} = 16}$$

15. (A)

His profit will be his income minus his expenses. He will earn $40 for each lawn, or 40$m$. He pays $35 is expenses each week, or 35x.
$$\textbf{profit = 40\textit{m} − 35\textit{x}}$$

16. (C)

$23 \div 4 = 5.75$ pizzas
Round up to **6 pizzas**.

17. (C)

Use the formula for percent change.
$$percent\ change = \frac{amount\ of\ change}{original\ amount}$$
$$= \frac{680 − 425}{425}$$
$$= \frac{255}{425} = 0.60 = \textbf{60\%}$$

18. (C)

Use the formula for percentages.
$$whole = \frac{part}{percent} = \frac{meal + tax}{1 + 0.0825}$$
$$= \frac{24.65}{1.0825} = \textbf{\$22.77}$$

19. (A)

Use the formula for percentages to find the number of games the team won.

part = $whole \times percent =$
$12 \times 0.75 = 9$

Subtract the number of games won from the games played to find the number of games the team lost.
$12 − 9 = \textbf{3}$

20. (D)

To estimate the amount of the change, round the price of each item to the nearest dollar amount and subtract from the total.
$\$50 − (\$13 + \$12 + \$4 + \$6)$
$= \$50 − \$35 = \textbf{\$15}$

21. (E)

Assign variables and write the ratios as fractions. Then, cross-multiply to solve for the number of apples and oranges sold.

x = apples
$$\frac{apples}{bananas} = \frac{3}{2} = \frac{x}{20}$$
$$60 = 2x$$
$$x = 30\ apples$$

y = oranges
$$\frac{oranges}{bananas} = \frac{1}{2} = \frac{y}{20}$$
$$2y = 20$$
$$y = 10\ oranges$$

To find the total, add the number of apples, oranges, and bananas together. $30 + 20 + 10 = \textbf{60 pieces of fruit}$

22. (E)

Set up an equation to find the number of people wearing neither white nor blue. Subtract the number of people wearing both colors so they are not counted twice.
$21 = 7 + 6 + neither − 5$
$neither = \textbf{13}$

23. (B)

Find the 5th term.
$−9 − (−36) = 27$
$27 \times −3 = −81$
Find the 6th term.
$−36 − (−81) = 45$
$45 \times −3 = \textbf{−135}$

24. (D)

Use the formula for the area of a rectangle to find the increase in its size.

$A = lw$

$A = (1.4l)(0.6w)$

$A = 0.84lw$

The new area will be 84% of the original area, a decrease of **16%**.

25. (C)

Set up a proportion and solve.

$$\frac{2775 \text{ miles}}{3 \text{ hr}} = \frac{x \text{ miles}}{5 \text{ hr}}$$

$2775(5) = 3x$

$x = \textbf{4625 miles}$

WORD KNOWLEDGE

1. **(A)**

   The word root *pax* means "peace," and the suffix *–ify* means "to cause to become more," and so, to pacify someone means to cause that person to become more peaceful, or to soothe him.

2. **(C)**

   An indolent person is lazy and avoids activity or exertion.

3. **(D)**

   The word root in the nouns *arson* and *ardor* means "to burn," and the suffix *–ent* means "doing a certain action," and so an ardent person burns with passion.

4. **(E)**

   Someone with a smiling countenance has a smile on her face.

5. **(E)**

   Someone with charisma, or charm, is attractive to others.

6. **(C)**

   To daunt means to intimidate or make someone apprehensive. For example, difficult tests are daunting to most people.

7. **(A)**

   The word root *crēdere* means "to believe," and the suffix *–ous* means "possessing or full of," so a credulous person is naïve enough to believe almost everything he hears or reads.

8. **(A)**

   A labyrinth is a maze or intricate pathway. Once someone enters a labyrinth, she can find it very difficult to find the way out.

9. **(E)**

   The word root *sacrō sānctus* means "made holy by sacred rites." Related words include *sacred, sacrifice, sanction,* and *sanctuary*.

10. **(B)**

    Rudimentary means "basic or elementary." For example, familiarity with the alphabet is a rudimentary reading skill that children learn at a young age.

11. **(C)**

    The prefix *im–* means "not," and the word root *parcial* means "biased," so an impartial jury is one whose members are not biased and are therefore able to evaluate evidence in an objective, unprejudiced manner.

12. **(B)**

    Reiterate means "to do something over again." For example, when someone reiterates a piece of information, she restates it.

13. **(D)**

    The prefix *pre–* means "before," the word root *cede* means "to go," and the suffix *–ent* means "something that," so a precedent is an event or action that comes before another event or action. A model comes first and is used as a plan to make something else.

14. **(A)**

    Prudent means "wise or judicious." For example, a prudent decision is a wise, practical one.

15. **(C)**

    The word root *figūrāre* means "to shape," and the suffix *–ive* means "indicating a tendency," so a figurative expression, or figure of speech, is shaped or invented rather than based on literal truth.

16. (C)

Innocuous means "harmless or inoffensive." For example, an innocuous substance is not harmful.

17. (C)

The word root *neglegere* means "to neglect," and the suffix root *–ence* means "the act of," so negligence is the act of neglecting—not paying proper attention to—someone or something.

18. (E)

Lax means "loose or open." For example, a lax set of rules would be permissive.

19. (A)

The word root *equi* means "equal," the word root *vōx* means "voice," and the suffix *–ate* means "perform the action of." Thus, to equivocate means to avoid privileging one explanation over another or giving a direct answer.

20. (E)

Ponderous means "very heavy or unwieldy." For example, a huge land animal such as an elephant has a lumbering, ponderous gait.

21. (C)

The word root *circum* means "around," and the word root *specere* means "to look," so a circumspect person looks cautiously around herself—considers her next step—in a self-protective way.

22. (E)

Assiduous means "to show great care or effort." For example, an assiduous person works hard.

23. (A)

Solicitous means "full of concern." For example, good waiters and waitresses are solicitous: they care about keeping their customers happy.

24. (C)

Aptitude means "natural ability or tendency." For example, someone with an aptitude for math can learn mathematical concepts quickly and easily.

25. (B)

The word root *jeu* or *jocus* means "play, game, or joke" and the word root *partir* means "to divide." A divided game is a game of chance that involves great risk, so to be in jeopardy means to be in danger (of losing).

MATH KNOWLEDGE

1. **(D)**

Simplify using PEMDAS.

$z^3(z + 2)^2 - 4z^3 + 2$

$z^3(z^2 + 4z + 4) - 4z^3 + 2$

$z^5 + 4z^4 + 4z^3 - 4z^3 + 2$

$\mathbf{z^5 + 4z^4 + 2}$

2. **(B)**

Use the rules of exponents to simplify the expression.

$\frac{(3x^2y^2)^2}{3^3x^{-2}y^3} = \frac{3^2x^4y^4}{3^3x^{-2}y^3} = \frac{x^6y}{3}$

3. **(A)**

$\left(\frac{1}{2}\right)^3 = \frac{1}{2} \times \frac{1}{2} \times \frac{1}{2} = \frac{1}{8}$

4. **(C)**

Use the formula for the area of a cylinder.

$V = \pi r^2 h$

$= \pi(4^2)(0.5) = \mathbf{25.12 \ ft^3}$

5. **(A)**

(A) Corresponding angles in right triangles are not necessarily the same, so they do not have to be similar.

(B) All spheres are similar.

(C) Corresponding angles in 30–60–90 triangles are the same, so all 30–60–90 triangles are similar.

(D) Corresponding angles in a square are all the same (90°), so all squares are similar.

(E) All corresponding angles in cubes are congruent, so they are all similar.

6. **(B)**

The slope 0.0293 gives the increase in passenger car miles (in billions) for each year that passes. Muliply this value by 5 to find the increase that occurs over 5 years: 5(0.0293) = **0.1465 billion miles**.

7. **(A)**

Simplify each root and add.

$\sqrt[3]{64} = 4$

$\sqrt[3]{729} = 9$

$4 + 9 = \mathbf{13}$

8. **(B)**

Find the highest possible multiple of 4 that is less than or equal to 397, and then subtract to find the remainder.

$99 \times 4 = 396$

$397 - 396 = \mathbf{1}$

9. **(D)**

Use the equation for tangent.

$\tan 50° = \frac{x}{300}$

$x = 300(\tan 50°)$

$\mathbf{x \approx 357}$

10. **(D)**

Use FOIL to multiply the first two terms.

$(x + 3)(x - 2) = x^2 + 3x - 2x - 6$

$= x^2 + x - 6$

Multiply the resulting trinomial by $(x + 4)$.

$(x^2 + x - 6)(x + 4) =$

$x^3 + 4x^2 + x^2 + 4x - 6x - 24$

$= \mathbf{x^3 + 5x^2 - 2x - 24}$

11. **(C)**

Plug each value into the equation.

$4(3 + 4)^2 - 4(3)^2 + 20 = 180 \neq 276$

$4(4 + 4)^2 - 4(3)^2 + 20 = 240 \neq 276$

$4(6 + 4)^2 - 4(6)^2 + 20 = \mathbf{276}$

$4(12 + 4)^2 - 4(12)^2 + 20 = 468 \neq 276$

$4(24 + 4)^2 - 4(24)^2 + 20 = 852 \neq 276$

12. **(A)**

Plug 0 in for y and solve for x.

$10x + 10y = 10$

$10x + 10(0) = 10$

$x = 1$

The x-intercept is at **(1, 0)**.

13. **(C)**

Round each value and add.

$129{,}113 \approx 129{,}000$
$34{,}602 \approx 35{,}000$
$129{,}000 + 35{,}000 = \textbf{164{,}000}$

14. (C)

Factor the trinomial and set each factor equal to 0.

$x^2 - 3x - 18 = 0$

$(x + 3)(x - 6) = 0$

$(x + 3) = 0$

$\boldsymbol{x = -3}$

$(x - 6) = 0$

$\boldsymbol{x = 6}$

15. (A)

Use the midpoint formula to find point B.

$M_x\colon \dfrac{(7 + x)}{2} = -3$

$x = -13$

$M_y\colon \dfrac{(12 + y)}{2} = 10$

$y = 8$

$B = \boldsymbol{(-13, 8)}$

16. (B)

Use the triangle inequality theorem to find the possible values for the third side, then calculate the possible perimeters.

$13 - 5 < s < 13 + 5$

$8 < s < 18$

$13 + 5 + 8 < P < 13 + 5 + 18$

$26 < P < 36$

26.5 is the only answer choice in this range

17. (E)

$5 \div 8 = 0.625$

$0.625 \times 100 = \textbf{62.5\%}$

18. (E)

Solve the system using substitution.

$z - 2x = 14 \rightarrow z = 2x + 14$

$2z - 6x = 18$

$2(2x + 14) - 6x = 18$

$4x + 28 - 6x = 18$

$-2x = -10$

$x = 5$

$z - 2(5) = 14$

$\boldsymbol{z = 24}$

19. (D)

Plug $m = 3$ and $n = -4$ into the expression and simplify.

$15m + 2n^2 - 7 =$

$15(3) + 2(-4)^2 - 7 = \textbf{70}$

20. (C)

Write out each number to find the largest.

A. 9299 ones $= 9299$

B. 903 tens $= 9030$

C. 93 hundreds $= \textbf{9300}$

D. 9 thousands $= 9000$

E. 9 thousandths $= 0.009$

21. (A)

Use the points to find the slope.

$m = \dfrac{y_2 - y_1}{x_2 - x_1} = \dfrac{-3 - 9}{4 - (-2)} = -2$

Use the point-slope equation to find the equation of the line.

$(y - y_1) = m(x - x_1)$

$y - (-3) = -2(x - 4)$

$\boldsymbol{y = -2x + 5}$

22. (E)

All the points lie on the circle, so each line segment is a radius. The sum of the 4 lines will be 4 times the radius.

$r = \dfrac{75}{2} = 37.5$

$4r = \textbf{150}$

23. (B)

Add 5 to each side to isolate the variable k.

$10 \leq k - 5$

$15 \leq k$

$\boldsymbol{k \geq 15}$

24. (B)

Calculate the volume of water in tank A.

$V = l \times w \times h$

$5 \times 10 \times 1 = 50\ \text{ft}^3$

Find the height this volume would reach in tank B.

$V = l \times w \times h$

$50 = 5 \times 5 \times h$

$h = \textbf{2 ft}$

25. **(B)**

Plug each set of values into the inequality $2a - 5b > 12$ and simplify.

(A) $2(2) - 5(6) = -26 \not> 12$

(B) $2(1) - 5(-3) = \textbf{17} > \textbf{12}$

(C) $2(-1) - 5(3) = -17 \not> 12$

(D) $2(7) - 5(2) = 4 \not> 12$

(E) $2(2) - 5(-1) = 9 \not> 12$

READING COMPREHENSION

1. **(A)**

   (A) is correct. The author writes that "the resulting war brought all these various actors, motivations, and agendas into a conflict in which no clear winner would emerge."

   (B) is incorrect. While the author does discuss the different actors, this is not the main idea of the passage.

   (C) is incorrect. The author describes the many other actors involved in the war but does not indicate that any actor was more involved than the Koreans themselves.

   (D) is incorrect. Though this is stated in the passage, it is not the main idea.

   (E) is incorrect. Though this is discussed in the last paragraph, it is not the main idea.

2. **(D)**

   (A) is incorrect. The text does not describe Japan's views on the spread of communism.

   (B) is incorrect. The text states that it was the rise of Mao Zedong to power in China that threatened America's global influence and power.

   (C) is incorrect. The text discusses American efforts to remove hundreds of thousands of Japanese soldiers and citizens but does not identify them as a threat.

   (D) is correct. The text describes Japan's "aggressive imperialism" as well as its colonization of Korea.

   (E) is incorrect. The text states that the exiled government was supported by the United States, not by Japan.

3. **(B)**

   (A) is incorrect. While the text references a communist government in the north and a communist group in the south, it does not discuss the preference of most Koreans.

   (B) is correct. Although the Soviet Union and the United States were willing to compromise over Korea in 1945, the text later states that by 1950 the two countries were at war due to each other's aggression.

   (C) is incorrect. The text states that Kim Il-sung was "reluctantly backed by China" but does not mention Mao Zedong's influence on the leader.

   (D) is incorrect. The text does not address Koreans' feelings about the US occupation of Japan.

   (E) is incorrect. The text does state that the Soviet Union controlled the area containing most of Korea's industrial resources; however, it does not explain what the Soviet Union did with those resources.

4. **(E)**

   (A) is incorrect. While the text does address this, it is not the primary purpose.

   (B) is incorrect. The text examines the causes of the war rather than its impact.

   (C) is incorrect. The text does not explain the events leading up to the war.

   (D) is incorrect. The text names only two leaders involved in the war, and they are not the primary purpose of the passage.

   (E) is correct. The first sentence states "Much of the complexity of the Korean War derives from the very different perspectives of the participants."

5. **(C)**

(A) is incorrect. In the second paragraph, the author writes, "In 1945, the Soviets… seized control of Korea. When the war ended, the United States . . . sent an expeditionary force to southern Korea."

(B) is incorrect. In the sixth paragraph, the author writes, "However, the scarce arable land and two-thirds of the people were in the southern zone."

(C) is correct. The United States and the Soviet Union agreed to *temporarily* divide Korea.

(D) is incorrect. In the sixth paragraph, the author writes that Korea "had been occupied by Japan for much of its history, making it automatically resistant to the interference of both Soviet and American troops."

(E) is incorrect. In the fifth paragraph, the author writes that a "second Chinese government persisted, exiled to Taiwan but politically sanctioned by the United States."

6. **(D)**

(A) is incorrect. While the author explains that Japan was a concern for Asian countries, there is no connection between US policy in Japan and Chinese actions.

(B) is incorrect. The text describes the Soviet Union encouraging aggression by North Korea, which would lead to a conflict with the United States.

(C) is incorrect. The text does not indicate that Japanese occupation created political or economic problems for Korea.

(D) is correct. The author describes several actions taken by the United States and the Soviet Union—namely the division of Korea—which created the internal conflict that resulted in war.

(E) is incorrect. The text describes Kim Il-sung's motivation as reuniting the country, rather than pursuing economic growth.

7. **(E)**

(A) is incorrect. The passage does not explain why the United States became involved in Somalia.

(B) is incorrect. While the passage does address this, it is not the primary purpose.

(C) is incorrect. The passage mentions this in the last paragraph, but it is not the primary purpose of the passage.

(D) is incorrect. The passage does mention the Rangers leaving behind supplies, but this is not the primary purpose of the passage.

(E) is correct. The passage identifies the reasons why the mission went awry and then explains how it led to changes in military operations and planning.

8. **(B)**

(A) is incorrect. The passage does not describe which parts of the US forces were most responsible for civilian deaths.

(B) is correct. The passage states that "they knew that the US would use the helicopters for air support during the raid… They also knew that American policy was to rescue the helicopter crew once it was downed, which gave the SNA the tactical advantage."

(C) is incorrect. While the passage does describe the densely populated city, it does not discuss any failed attempts at landing.

(D) is incorrect. The passage does state that the SNA targeted the helicopters but not that the weapons were specifically designed for that purpose.

(E) is incorrect. The passage does not discuss the noise of the helicopters.

9. **(C)**

    (A) is incorrect. The passage states that the center of Aidid's territory was the capital of Mogadishu.

    (B) is incorrect. The passage describes how Aidid and his people studied US tactical patterns and developed strategies in response.

    (C) is correct. The passage states, "raids [were planned] to capture key members of the various factions that were causing the most strife and conflict, with particular focus on the Somali National Alliance."

    (D) is incorrect. There is no evidence in the passage that Aidid wanted to preserve any US military technology.

    (E) is incorrect. The passage describes the civil war as the result of multiple competing warlords, and it does not ever state that any others were interested in peace.

10. **(A)**

    (A) is correct. The passage states that "public outrage ultimately led to American withdrawal from Somalia altogether and to the country's descent into deeper chaos."

    (B) is incorrect. The passage states, "(2) they occurred under the cover of night."

    (C) is incorrect. The passage states that "the mission was ultimately successful in obtaining its targets" despite its outcome.

    (D) is incorrect. The passage states, "Because of the deeply fractured nature of the country at the time, the US mission was a daunting task without a clear goal."

    (E) is incorrect. The passage states that "the Rangers were bogged down by gunfire on the streets, and the two Black Hawk helicopters providing support were shot down."

11. **(D)**

    (A) is incorrect. The author argues that "there is no surefire way to be successful in urban warfare."

    (B) is incorrect. The passage does not discuss past wars in urban settings, only US raid tactics.

    (C) is incorrect. The author states that civilian deaths were high because combatants were able to move in and out of the general population easily because of the density. Advanced technology is not mentioned as an issue.

    (D) is correct. The passage states that "deep complexities of urban warfare . . . led to increased focus on improving information gathering, developing ways of observing targets from a safe distance, and creating more flexible and thorough plans for urban missions."

    (E) is incorrect. The passage describes the difficulty of keeping military secrets in Mogadishu because of the base of operations at the airport.

12. **(A)**

    (A) is correct. The "collateral" refers to civilians, who were killed in addition to the soldiers.

    (B) is incorrect. There is no context that implies that the deaths were only about native-born people.

    (C) is incorrect. There is no context that implies whether the deaths were intended or not intended.

    (D) is incorrect. There is no context that implies the word is about the value of the deaths.

    (E) is incorrect. There is no context related to how the deaths were perceived by others.

13. **(D)**

(A) is incorrect. Washington emphasizes that his argument is "not be understood as capable of patronizing infidelity to existing engagements... [L]et those engagements be observed in their genuine sense." He argues that America should avoid future entanglements but indicates that the country should not break from its existing relationships.

(B) is incorrect. Washington states, "It is our true policy to steer clear of permanent alliances with any portion of the foreign world; so far, I mean, as we are now at liberty to do it[...]"

(C) is incorrect. Washington states, "Hence, therefore, it must be unwise in us to implicate ourselves, by artificial ties, in the ordinary vicissitudes of her [Europe's] politics, or the ordinary combinations and collisions of her friendships or enmities."

(D) is correct. The author writes, "It is our true policy to steer clear of permanent alliances with any portion of the foreign world; so far, I mean, as we are now at liberty to do it[...]"

(E) Incorrect. Washington advocates specifically for a policy of isolationism.

14. **(A)**

(A) is correct. Washington states that Europe is "engaged in frequent controversies" and that it would be "unwise to implicate ourselves...in the ordinary vicissitudes of her politics, or the ordinary combinations and collisions of her friendships and enmities."

(B) is incorrect. This answer choice does not fit in the context of the sentence.

(C) is incorrect. Washington's use of the description "the ordinary combinations and collisions of her friendships and enmities" suggests that European politics are regularly fluctuating, not just mutating in the current moment.

(D) is incorrect. Washington's description of European politics indicates that they are fluctuating, not remaining stagnant.

(E) is incorrect. Washington does not allude to rules or laws in European politics.

15. **(A)**

(A) is correct. The passage indicates that snakes' "intricate diamonds, stripes, and swirls help the animals hide from predators, but perhaps most importantly (for us humans, anyway), the markings can also indicate whether the snake is venomous."

(B) is incorrect. Though the author does mention one difference between the kingsnake and the coral snake, this is not the primary purpose of the passage.

(C) is incorrect. The author does not indicate why snakes are dangerous, only that some of them are.

(D) is incorrect. Though the author does provide some examples of this, this answer choice is more general, while the passage focused on snakes in particular.

(E) is incorrect. While the author may be contradicting readers' understanding of the species, this is not the primary purpose of the passage.

16. **(B)**

(A) is incorrect. The author mentions that "the kingsnake is actually nonvenomous" but provides no more information about whether the kingsnake poses a danger to humans.

(B) is correct. The final paragraph of the passage states that the two species "frequently [share] a habitat" and that "[a] predatory hawk or eagle, usually hunting from high in the sky, can't tell the difference between the two species, and so the kingsnake gets passed over and lives another day."

(C) is incorrect. The author does not imply that it is easy to tell the difference between venomous and nonvenomous snakes, only that it is possible.

(D) is incorrect. The final paragraph states that the kingsnake "has very similar marking to the venomous coral snake" and does not indicate that these markings change with circumstances.

(E) is incorrect. The author mentions that "the kingsnake is actually nonvenomous" but provides no more information about whether the kingsnake poses a danger to humans.

17. **(C)**

(A) is incorrect. The second paragraph states that "[a] predatory hawk or eagle, usually hunting from high in the sky, can't tell the difference between the two species, and so the kingsnake gets passed over and lives another day."

(B) is incorrect. The second paragraph states that "[t]he scarlet kingsnake, for example, has very similar markings to the venomous coral snake with whom it frequently shares a habitat."

(C) is correct. The first paragraph states that "[w]hile it might seem counterintuitive for a venomous snake to stand out in bright red or blue, that fancy costume tells any nearby predator that approaching him would be a bad idea." The coral snake's markings do not allow it to hide from predators but rather to "ward [them] off[.]"

(D) is incorrect. The second paragraph states that "the kingsnake is actually nonvenomous; it's merely pretending to be dangerous to eat."

(E) is incorrect. The first paragraph states that snakes' "intricate diamonds, stripes, and swirls help the animals hide from predators[.]"

18. **(A)**

(A) is correct. The passage states that "intricate diamonds, stripes, and swirls help the animals hide from predators[,]" implying that these markings are complex enough to allow the animals to blend in with their surroundings.

(B) is incorrect. The passage indicates that colorful markings do not allow the animals to hide but rather to ward off predators, so the word *colorful* does not apply in the context of the sentence.

(C) is incorrect. This answer choice does not fit in the context of the sentence, as the animals do not choose their markings.

(D) is incorrect. The author does not suggest that animals' markings are changeable.

(E) is incorrect. This answer choice does not fit in the context of the sentence.

19. **(C)**

(A) is incorrect. The second paragraph states that "[t]he scarlet kingsnake, for example, has very similar markings to the venomous coral snake with whom it frequently shares a habitat. However, the kingsnake is actually nonvenomous[.]"

(B) is incorrect. The second paragraph states that "[t]he scarlet kingsnake, for example, has very similar markings to the venomous coral snake with whom it frequently shares a habitat. However, the kingsnake is actually nonvenomous[.]"

(C) is correct. The second paragraph states that "[t]he scarlet kingsnake, for example, has very similar markings to the venomous coral snake with whom it frequently shares a habitat. However, the kingsnake is actually nonvenomous[.]"

(D) is incorrect. The second paragraph states that "[t]he scarlet kingsnake, for example, has very similar markings to the venomous coral snake with whom it frequently shares a habitat. However, the kingsnake is actually nonvenomous[.]"

(E) is incorrect. The second paragraph states that "[t]he scarlet kingsnake, for example, has very similar markings to the venomous coral snake with whom it frequently shares a habitat. However, the kingsnake is actually nonvenomous[.]"

20. **(D)**

(A) is incorrect. The author includes nothing to suggest that hand sanitizer disguises pathogens.

(B) is incorrect. The author includes nothing to suggest that hand sanitizer hides pathogens.

(C) is incorrect. The author notes that while hand sanitizer kills most of the bacteria on the surface of the hands, it "does nothing to remove organic matter" from them.

(D) is correct. The author writes that "hands 'cleaned' with hand sanitizer may still harbor pathogens" because sanitizer "does nothing to remove organic matter" from the hands. The bacteria are not completely washed off, and therefore some are able to continue living on the surface of the hands.

(E) is incorrect. The author includes nothing to suggest that hand sanitizer breeds pathogens.

21. **(B)**

(A) is incorrect. In the first paragraph, the author writes, "Many illnesses are spread when people touch infected surfaces, such as door handles or other people's hands, and then touch their own eyes, mouths, or noses."

(B) is correct. In the second paragraph, the author writes, "The [hand washing] process doesn't even require warm water—studies have shown that cold water is just as effective at reducing the number of microbes on the hands. Antibacterial soaps are also available, although several studies have shown that simple soap and cold water is just as effective."

(C) is incorrect. In the third paragraph, the author writes, "These gels, liquids, and foams contain a high concentration of alcohol (usually at least 60 percent) that kills most bacteria and fungi; they can also be effective against some, but not all, viruses."

(D) is incorrect. In the final paragraph, the author writes, "Thus, while hand sanitizer can be helpful in situations where soap and clean water aren't available, a simple hand washing is still the best option."

(E) is incorrect. In the third paragraph, the author writes, "There is a downside to hand sanitizer, however. Because the sanitizer isn't rinsed from hands, it only kills pathogens and does nothing to remove organic matter. So, hands 'cleaned' with hand sanitizer may still harbor pathogens."

22. **(B)**

(A) is incorrect. The author includes nothing to suggest that water has antibacterial properties.

(B) is correct. The author writes that because hand sanitizer "isn't rinsed from hands [as is water], it only kills pathogens and does nothing to remove organic matter."

(C) is incorrect. The author writes, "The [hand washing] process doesn't even require warm water—studies have shown that cold water is just as effective at reducing the number of microbes on the hands. Antibacterial soaps are also available, although several studies have shown that simple soap and cold water are just as effective." This implies that the temperature of the water is unrelated to its effectiveness.

(D) is incorrect. The author indicates that the temperature of the water is unrelated to its effectiveness (see C above).

(E) is incorrect. The passage does not discuss hydrating the skin.

23. (C)

(A) is incorrect. While both of these details are included in the passage, they do not provide an adequate summary of the passage overall.

(B) is incorrect. While both of these details are included in the passage, they do not provide an adequate summary of the passage overall.

(C) is correct. Together, these sentences provide an adequate summary of the passage overall.

(D) is incorrect. While both of these details are included in the passage, they do not provide an adequate summary of the passage overall.

(E) is incorrect. While both of these details are included in the passage, they do not provide an adequate summary of the passage overall.

24. (A)

(A) is correct. Each paragraph examines hand washing from a different angle.

(B) is incorrect. In the final paragraph, the author writes, "Thus, while hand sanitizer can be helpful in situations where soap and clean water aren't available, a simple hand washing is still the best option." The author acknowledges that hand sanitizer is a viable option when soap and water are unavailable.

(C) is incorrect. Though the author lists a few of the diseases that are spread through daily interaction "including ... the flu, the common cold, diarrhea, and many acute respiratory illnesses[,]" she does not explain any further.

(D) is incorrect. While the author does explain how hand washing and hand sanitizer are effective, her goal is not just to describe hand washing, but rather to convince readers of its importance.

(E) is incorrect. The author writes, "Antibacterial soaps are also available, although several studies have shown that simple soap and cold water are just as effective[,]" but this is the extent of her comment on antibacterial soaps; she does not take a particular stance against them or tell readers not to purchase them.

25. (A)

(A) is correct. In the first paragraph, the author writes, "Many illnesses are spread when people touch infected surfaces, such as door handles or other people's hands, and then touch their own eyes, mouths, or noses." The reader can infer from this sentence that hand washing prevents the spread of surface-borne illnesses.

(B) is incorrect. The author says that "[m]any illnesses are spread" when people touch their "eyes, mouths, and noses[,]" but not all illnesses; thus the reader can infer that hand washing is not solely for people who touch their faces.

(C) is incorrect. The author says that "while hand sanitizer can be helpful in situations where soap and clean water aren't available, a simple hand washing is still the best option." Thus, hand sanitizer should be not used instead of hand washing altogether, but it does effectively serve its purpose as an alternative when soap and water are not available.

(D) is incorrect. The author indicates that hand sanitizer will not replace hand washing altogether because it "does nothing to remove organic matter" from hands after use. Thus, "hands 'cleaned' with hand sanitizer may still harbor pathogens."

(E) is incorrect. The author writes that "if pathogens can be removed from the hands before they spread, infections can be prevented." This implies that healthy people should wash their hands as well to prevent the spread of disease from surfaces they have touched.

PHYSICAL SCIENCE

1. **(D)**

   (A) is incorrect. Power is a measure of the rate at which work is done.

   (B) is incorrect. A force is a push or pull that changes an object's velocity.

   (C) is incorrect. Displacement is the distance between an object's start and end positions.

   (D) is correct. Acceleration is the rate at which velocity changes.

   (E) is incorrect. Energy is the measure of an object's capacity to do work.

2. **(B)**

   (A) is incorrect. The magnitude of an earthquake does not directly refer to its power; rather, it refers to the energy released during the earthquake.

   (B) is correct. The magnitude of an earthquake refers to the energy released during the earthquake.

   (C) is incorrect. The magnitude of an earthquake does not directly refer to its destructive ability; however this is indirectly related due to the impact of the energy released during the earthquake.

   (D) is incorrect. The magnitude of an earthquake does not directly refer to its depth, though the depth of an earthquake can affect its magnitude.

   (E) is incorrect. The magnitude of an earthquake does not describe the location of an earthquake.

3. **(B)**

   (A) is incorrect. A solar eclipse is when the moon moves between the sun and Earth.

   (B) is correct. A lunar eclipse is when Earth moves between the moon and the sun.

   (C) is incorrect. A black hole is a collapsed star with tremendous gravitational pull.

   (D) is incorrect. A supernova is an explosion of the core of a star.

   (E) is incorrect. An aurora occurs when solar winds interact with the Earth's magnetic field.

4. **(D)**

   (A) is incorrect. In a substitution reaction, a single atom or ion swaps places with another atom or ion.

   (B) is incorrect. In an acid-base reaction, an acid and a base react to neutralize each other. This reaction does not include an acid or base.

   (C) is incorrect. In a decomposition reaction, a compound breaks down into smaller molecules or compounds.

   (D) is correct. Combustion is defined as a reaction in which a hydrocarbon reacts with O_2 to produce CO_2 and H_2O.

   (E) is incorrect. In a synthesis reaction, two or more reactants combine to form a single product.

5. **(A)**

   (A) is correct. Friction is a force that opposes motion.

   (B) is incorrect. Friction works in the direction opposite an object's motion, so it will not push down on a surface.

   (C) is incorrect. Torque is the force that creates rotational motion.

   (D) is incorrect. Friction generally works against the force of gravity.

   (E) is incorrect. Friction may work with or against the normal force.

6. **(E)**

   (A) is incorrect. Wavelength is the distance between cycles of a wave. It does not affect how large an object appears to be.

   (B) is incorrect. Diffraction occurs when waves pass through a narrow opening and then spread out.

   (C) is incorrect. Amplitude is the height of a wave; it affects how loud a sound is perceived to be.

(D) is incorrect. Reflection occurs when waves bounce off an object. When light waves are reflected, it does not change the apparent size of an object being viewed.

(E) is correct. Lenses refract, or bend, light waves to make objects appear larger.

7. **(C)**

(A) is incorrect. Isotopes must have the same number of protons, not electrons.

(B) is incorrect. Isotopes are defined as having different numbers of neutrons, not the same number.

(C) is correct. Isotopes are atoms of the same element with the same number of protons but different numbers of neutrons.

(D) is incorrect. Isotopes have the same number of protons but can also have the same number of electrons.

(E) is incorrect. Atoms with different numbers of protons would not be the same element.

8. **(A)**

(A) is correct. Tension is the force that results from objects being pulled or hung.

(B) is incorrect. The box experiences friction as it slides against the ramp.

(C) is incorrect. Gravity is the force pulling the box down the ramp.

(D) is incorrect. The normal force is the upward force of the ramp on the box.

(E) is incorrect. The buoyant force is the upward force experienced by floating objects.

9. **(E)**

(A) is incorrect. The lithosphere is the rigid outermost layer of the earth.

(B) is incorrect. The asthenosphere lies beneath the lithosphere and is mostly solid.

(C) is incorrect. The mesosphere lies beneath the asthenosphere and is mostly solid.

(D) is incorrect. The inner core is solid and composed primarily of iron.

(E) is correct. The outer core is composed of a liquid, iron-nickel alloy and flows around the inner core.

10. **(B)**

(A) is incorrect. Particles in a liquid are more tightly packed than particles in a gas, but there is more space among particles in a liquid than among them in a solid.

(B) is correct. Gas is the state of matter in which atomic particles are most loosely packed, and the greatest amount of space exists among atoms.

(C) is incorrect. Particles are most tightly packed in a solid.

(D) is incorrect. The nuclei within a plasma are electrically charged, and electrons move about freely.

(E) is incorrect. A crystal is a type of solid in which atoms are arranged in a rigid structure.

11. **(B)**

(A) is incorrect. Mercury is the planet closest to the sun. Venus orbits between Mercury and Earth.

(B) is correct. Venus's orbit is closest to Earth. Venus is the second planet from the sun, and Earth is the third planet from the sun.

(C) is incorrect. Jupiter is the fifth planet from the sun.

(D) is incorrect. Saturn is the sixth planet from the sun.

(E) is incorrect. Neptune is the farthest planet from the sun.

12. **(C)**

(A) is incorrect. An atom with a charge of $-17e$ would have seventeen more electrons than protons.

(B) is incorrect. An atom with a charge of $-7e$ would have seven more electrons than protons.

(C) is correct. This atom has a total charge of $-5e + 12e = +7e$.

(D) is incorrect. An atom with a charge of +17 would have seventeen more protons than electrons.

(E) is incorrect. Neutral atoms have an equal number of electrons and protons.

13. (B)

(A) is incorrect. A mineral is a naturally occurring substance.

(B) is correct. A mineral is inorganic; only a rock may be composed of organic material.

(C) is incorrect. A mineral is a solid.

(D) is incorrect. A mineral has a crystalline structure.

(E) is incorrect. A mineral is composed of a single chemical compound.

14. (A)

(A) is correct. When water changes form, it does not change the chemical composition of the substance. Once water becomes ice, the ice can easily turn back into water.

(B) is incorrect. During a chemical change, the chemical composition of the substance changes and cannot be reversed. Baking a cake is an example of a chemical change.

(C) is incorrect. Rusting is an example of a chemical change.

(D) is incorrect. Setting off fireworks causes a chemical change.

(E) is incorrect. Neutralizing an acid with a base is a chemical change.

15. (B)

(A) is incorrect. The mesosphere is the layer where the air becomes thin and has some of the coldest temperatures on Earth.

(B) is correct. The stratosphere contains a sublayer called the ozone layer, which absorbs harmful ultraviolet radiation from the sun.

(C) is incorrect. The troposphere is the layer closest to Earth's surface and is where most of Earth's weather occurs.

(D) is incorrect. The thermosphere contains molecules that are spread far apart and become super-heated.

(E) is incorrect. The exosphere is the outermost layer of the atmosphere and does not absorb ultraviolet radiation.

16. (A)

(A) is correct. The sun is about ninety-three million miles from Earth; the next closest star is about twenty-five trillion miles away.

(B) is incorrect. The moon orbits Earth.

(C) is incorrect. Earth is always closer to the sun than Jupiter is.

(D) is incorrect. Mercury is the closest planet to the sun, but Venus is closer to Earth.

(E) is incorrect. Uranus is farther from the sun than Jupiter.

17. (E)

(A) is incorrect. All mixtures, whether saturated or unsaturated, have a solute and solvent that are not chemically bonded.

(B) is incorrect. The state of the solute and solvent has no effect on whether the solution is saturated.

(C) is incorrect. A solution with an evenly distributed solute is homogeneous, and it may be saturated or unsaturated.

(D) is incorrect. A solute is always evenly distributed in a solution. This does not affect whether the solution is saturated.

(E) is correct. No more solute can be dissolved into a saturated solution.

18. (A)

(A) is correct. Geysers are caused by geothermal heating of water underground.

(B) is incorrect. Glaciers are formed when snow and ice do not melt before new layers of snow and ice are added.

(C) is incorrect. Tsunamis are caused by earthquakes on the ocean floor.

(D) is incorrect. Tornadoes are caused by instability of warm, humid air in the lower atmosphere mixing with cool air in the upper atmosphere.

(E) is incorrect. Hurricanes are powered by water evaporating from the ocean.

19. **(B)**

(A) is incorrect. Chemical potential energy is stored in the bonds between atoms.

(B) is correct. Elastic potential energy is stored by compressing or expanding an object.

(C) is incorrect. Gravitational potential energy is stored in objects that have been moved away from a gravitational mass.

(D) is incorrect. Electric potential energy is stored in charged objects.

(E) is incorrect. Kinetic energy is the energy of objects in motion.

20. **(B)**

(A) is incorrect. One hour is $\frac{1}{24}$ of the time it takes for the earth to rotate on its axis.

(B) is correct. Earth takes approximately twenty-four hours to rotate on its axis.

(C) is incorrect. The moon takes approximately one month to revolve around the Earth.

(D) is incorrect. The Earth takes approximately one year to revolve around the sun.

(E) is incorrect. A century is one hundred years.

TABLE READING

1.	(A)	21.	(D)
2.	(D)	22.	(B)
3.	(B)	23.	(C)
4.	(C)	24.	(A)
5.	(E)	25.	(E)
6.	(E)	26.	(C)
7.	(D)	27.	(B)
8.	(B)	28.	(B)
9.	(C)	29.	(C)
10.	(E)	30.	(C)
11.	(D)	31.	(D)
12.	(C)	32.	(A)
13.	(E)	33.	(B)
14.	(B)	34.	(C)
15.	(A)	35.	(D)
16.	(A)	36.	(B)
17.	(D)	37.	(E)
18.	(B)	38.	(A)
19.	(C)	39.	(D)
20.	(B)	40.	(C)

INSTRUMENT COMPREHENSION

1.	(C)	climbing	banking left	north
2.	(D)	level flight	no bank	west
3.	(C)	climbing	banking left	west
4.	(B)	level flight	no bank	north
5.	(A)	climbing	no bank	north
6.	(A)	climbing	banking left	east
7.	(D)	level flight	banking right	north
8.	(C)	descending	banking left	southeast
9.	(D)	level flight	banking left	south
10.	(C)	level flight	banking left	west
11.	(B)	descending	no bank	east
12.	(B)	level flight	banking right	west
13.	(C)	level flight	no bank	south
14.	(A)	level flight	no bank	east
15.	(A)	descending	banking right	southwest
16.	(B)	level flight	banking left	north
17.	(D)	descending	banking left	west
18.	(B)	descending	banking right	southeast
19.	(D)	climbing	banking left	east
20.	(A)	climbing	no bank	west
21.	(A)	climbing	banking right	west
22.	(B)	level flight	banking right	south
23.	(D)	climbing	banking right	north
24.	(D)	climbing	no bank	east
25.	(B)	descending	no bank	west

BLOCK COUNTING

1. (D)
2. (C)
3. (A)
4. (C)
5. (B)
6. (C)
7. (B)
8. (B)
9. (A)
10. (E)
11. (B)
12. (D)
13. (A)
14. (C)
15. (B)

16. (A)
17. (C)
18. (E)
19. (B)
20. (D)
21. (B)
22. (A)
23. (C)
24. (E)
25. (D)
26. (D)
27. (B)
28. (E)
29. (B)
30. (A)

Aviation Information

1. **(C)**

   (A) is incorrect. Ailerons require pilot input.

   (B) is incorrect. The nose of the aircraft rises when the tail is pushed down.

   (C) is correct. When the elevators are raised, the tail of the aircraft is pushed down, which increases the pitch and raises the nose of the aircraft.

   (D) is incorrect. The elevators do not control left turns.

   (E) is incorrect. The elevators do not control right turns.

2. **(C)**

   (A) is incorrect. The ailerons affect the longitudinal axis of the aircraft during turns.

   (B) is incorrect. The elevators affect pitch.

   (C) is correct. The rudder affects yaw; it controls the vertical axis of the aircraft.

   (D) is incorrect. The spoilers reduce lift, increase drag, and control speed.

   (E) is incorrect. The position of the wings adjusts the airflow pressure, controlling lift and drag.

3. **(B)**

   (A) is incorrect. The teeter hinge allows the blades to flap.

   (B) is correct. The swashplate allows for directional movement of the aircraft.

   (C) is incorrect. The ducted fan is a component of the NOTAR aircraft design.

   (D) is incorrect. The tail boom is a structural component that supports the tail rotor assembly.

   (E) is incorrect. The skids are used as landing gear for rotary-wing aircraft.

4. **(A)**

   (A) is correct. This climb is used to clear obstacles that may be in the flight path.

   (B) is incorrect. This climb is used to cover the most distance, not the most altitude.

   (C) is incorrect. This climb will not produce the greatest altitude.

   (D) is incorrect. This is not a type of climb.

   (E) is incorrect. This is not a type of climb.

5. **(D)**

   (A) is incorrect. The aircraft pitch would indeed change; however, this is not the best complete answer.

   (B) is incorrect. The airspeed would increase and the nose of the aircraft would pitch downward.

   (C) is incorrect. The airspeed would indeed increase due to the change of airflow around the wings caused by the cyclic or control wheel; however, this is not the best answer.

   (D) is correct. This is the best answer because it describes the combination of changes to the aircraft.

   (E) is incorrect. Changes in the foot pedals control the rudder, which affects any yawing of an aircraft.

6. **(B)**

   (A) is incorrect. A coaxial rotor system cancels torque effect by using counter rotating rotor heads.

   (B) is correct. Translating tendency causes a rotary-wing aircraft to drift laterally due to tail rotor thrust.

   (C) is incorrect. Gyroscopic precession is when a force input is applied yet the force output is felt 90 degrees later in the plane of rotation.

   (D) is incorrect. The tail rotor cancels out the torque effect.

   (E) is incorrect. An effective translational lift results from increased efficiency of the main rotor system as directional flight is established.

7. **(C)**

(A) is incorrect. A change of heading would not reduce airspeed.

(B) is incorrect. Decreasing altitude will result in an initial higher airspeed.

(C) is correct. Approaching the red line means the aircraft is reaching the maximum airspeed for the aircraft.

(D) is incorrect. Increasing airspeed will exceed the maximum airspeed of the aircraft.

(E) is incorrect. Increasing thrust will increase airspeed to an excess level if all other forces remain the same.

8. **(C)**

(A) is incorrect. Above ground level (AGL) is an altitude measurement.

(B is incorrect. Degrees are used in directional headings.

(C) is correct. Feet per minute (fpm) describes a rate of climb.

(D) is incorrect. Airspeed is measured in knots.

(E) is incorrect. Mean sea level (MSL) is an altitude measurement.

9. **(C)**

(A) is incorrect. The rudder controls adverse yaw.

(B) is incorrect. The wings and ailerons control bank.

(C) is correct. The lateral axis controls pitch when the nose moves up and down.

(D) is incorrect. The longitudinal axis controls roll.

(E) is incorrect. The vertical axis controls yaw.

10. **(C)**

(A) is incorrect. The teeter hinge allows the blades to flap.

(B) is incorrect. The rotor hub is the center attachment point for the rotor head components.

(C) is correct. The blade grips allow the main rotor blades to feather.

(D) is incorrect. The skids are used as landing gear for rotary-wing aircraft.

(E) is incorrect. The pitch horn couples the blade cuff to the pitch links.

11. **(E)**

(A) is incorrect. This describes indicated altitude.

(B) is incorrect. This describes pressure altitude.

(C) is incorrect. This describes density altitude.

(D) is incorrect. This describes true altitude.

(E) is correct. Absolute altitude is indeed the height above ground level (AGL).

12. **(A)**

(A) is correct. The angle of attack (AOA) is the angle between the chord (pitch) of the aircraft wing and the direction of relative wind.

(B) is incorrect. The artificial horizon is the line that represents the horizon of the earth and the aircraft attitude on the attitude indicator.

(C) is incorrect. The minimum limits of aircraft performance are shown on the vertical speed indicator.

(D) is incorrect. The pressure altitude is displayed on the altimeter when the setting window is adjusted to 29.92 Hg.

(E) is incorrect. A stall is when aircraft airspeed experiences decreased lift and lower airspeed, causing the AOA to be exceeded.

13. **(A)**

(A) is correct. The pilot must be acknowledged with the aircraft call sign to establish communications.

(B) is incorrect. This is true for Class C and D controlled airspaces but not true for Class B airspace.

(C) is incorrect. Approval for clearance is required for Class A through D controlled airspaces.

(D) is incorrect. When aircraft clearances are required, it applies to all types of aircraft.

(E) is incorrect. If clearance is required for entering an airspace, clearance is also required for exiting it.

14. **(D)**

(A) is incorrect. This would increase airspeed.

(B) is incorrect. This would increase airspeed.

(C) is incorrect. Extending the ailerons and flaps would decrease thrust, but this is done during landing to slow the aircraft.

(D) is correct. When increasing pitch, thrust must be increased to provide lift and maintain vertical speed or a stall will result.

(E) is incorrect. The rudder has no effect on thrust.

15. **(A)**

(A) is correct. This is the acronym for aircraft gross weight, also known as all-up weight (AUW). This weight changes during the flight due to consumables (i.e., oil and fuel).

(B) is incorrect. This is the acronym for maximum landing weight.

(C) is incorrect. This is maximum ramp weight.

(D) is incorrect. This is maximum takeoff weight.

(E) is incorrect. This is operating empty weight.

16. **(D)**

(A) is incorrect. A shallow turn is less than 20 degrees and does not need aileron pressure to return the aircraft to level flight, unlike medium and steep turns.

(B) is incorrect. While medium turns do require aileron pressure to return the aircraft to level flight, a shallow turn is less than 20 degrees and does not need aileron pressure to return the aircraft to level flight.

(C) is incorrect. A shallow turn is less than 20 degrees and does not need

aileron pressure to return the aircraft to level flight.

(D) is correct. These turns are between 20 and 45 degrees and greater than a 45-degree bank. The pilot inputs aileron pressure to return the aircraft to level flight for both of these types of turns.

(E) is incorrect. There is no such turn.

17. **(C)**

(A) is incorrect. Weight, lift, thrust, and drag must be in balance in order to hover.

(B) is incorrect. An effective translational lift results from increased efficiency of the main rotor system as directional flight is established.

(C) is correct. Advancing and retreating blades of the rotor system generate unequal lifting forces: a dissymmetry of lift.

(D) is incorrect. Gyroscopic precession is when a force input is applied yet the force output is felt 90 degrees later in the plane of rotation.

(E) is incorrect. Autorotation is when the rotor blades are driven by relative wind rather than by the aircraft's powerplant.

18. **(E)**

(A) is incorrect. The cyclic controls the pitch and roll axis of the aircraft.

(B) is incorrect. The collective changes the pitch of the blades simultaneously.

(C) is incorrect. The tail rotor pedals control the yaw axis of the aircraft.

(D) is incorrect. Translating tendency causes a rotary-wing aircraft to drift laterally due to tail rotor thrust.

(E) is correct. The throttle maintains the engine within optimal flight parameters.

19. **(D)**

(A) is incorrect. Lag has a delay of 6 to 9 seconds; trend information is in real time.

(B) is incorrect. Lag has a delay of 6 to 9 seconds.

(C) is incorrect. Although trend information is in real time, lag is not.

(D) is correct. Trend information displays in real time in relation to the movement of the cyclic.

(E) is incorrect. Trend information does display in real time.

20. **(C)**

(A) is incorrect. AOA is the angle between the direction of the airflow and the chord on a wing—the imaginary reference line that extends from the leading edge to the trailing edge.

(B) is incorrect. A degree is the directional measurement for an aircraft.

(C) is correct. Airspeed is measured in knots.

(D) is incorrect. Mean sea level (MSL) is an altitude measurement.

(E) is incorrect. Rate of climb is a type of climb performed to navigate above obstacles during takeoff.

PRACTICE TEST TWO

VERBAL ANALOGIES

This part of the test measures your ability to reason and see relationships among words. You are to choose the option that best completes the analogy developed at the beginning of each statement.

1. LABYRINTH is to MAZE as HIERARCHY is to
   - (A) ROOF
   - (B) PLANE
   - (C) LADDER
   - (D) LOWLINESS
   - (E) HEIGHT

2. TRIUMVIRATE is to 3 as
   - (A) KIDNEYS are to 2
   - (B) TWELVE is to 24
   - (C) SIX is to SEPTET
   - (D) EON is to ETERNITY
   - (E) QUARTET is to 4

3. STOMACH is to DIGESTION as LUNGS are to
   - (A) ORGAN
   - (B) SMOKING
   - (C) CHEST
   - (D) OXYGEN
   - (E) RESPIRATION

4. INEPTITUDE is to AMPLITUDE as
   - (A) INTRUSION is to INSCRIBE
   - (B) REASONABLE is to UNREASONING
   - (C) APPLIANCE is to APPLICATION
   - (D) COSTUME is to COSMOPOLITAN
   - (E) WISTFULNESS is to BLAMELESSNESS

5. FEELING is to FERVOR as OPINION is to
   - (A) HAPPINESS
   - (B) SORROW
   - (C) THOUGHT
   - (D) CONVICTION
   - (E) NOTION

6. BELITTLE is to PRAISE as GALVANIZE is to
   (A) BORE
   (B) ELECTRIFY
   (C) DISPARAGE
   (D) ENCOURAGE
   (E) ANIMATE

7. DISLIKE is to RANCOR as TIREDNESS is to
   (A) HATRED
   (B) ADORATION
   (C) EXHAUSTION
   (D) SLEEPINESS
   (E) IMPATIENCE

8. PEBBLE is to BOULDER as HUT is to
   (A) SHACK
   (B) BUILDING
   (C) COLOSSAL
   (D) NUGGET
   (E) CASTLE

9. INCH is to FOOT as CENTIMETER is to
   (A) METRIC
   (B) METER
   (C) LENGTH
   (D) SHORTER
   (E) RULER

10. FEW is to COUNTLESS as BRIEF is to
    (A) SHORT
    (B) MOMENTARY
    (C) UNDERSIZED
    (D) INTERMINABLE
    (E) OBNOXIOUS

11. ABBERATION is to DEVIATION as
    (A) DECADENCE is to THRIFTINESS
    (B) HEDONIST is to PLEASURE
    (C) ICONOCLAST is to REBEL
    (D) PARIAH is to SHUN
    (E) QUANDARY is to CERTAINTY

12. KNIFE is to SLICING as FORK is to
    (A) SLURPING
    (B) PIERCING
    (C) GORGING
    (D) SPOONING
    (E) PLUNGING

13. SENTENCE is to PARAGRAPH as STANZA is to
    (A) EDITORIAL
    (B) ESSAY
    (C) PLAY
    (D) POEM
    (E) LINE

14. EXCRUCIATING is to EXTRAORDINARY as
    (A) CONCIOUSNESS is to WARINESS
    (B) DESTRUCTION is to INSTRUCTION
    (C) UNSATISFACTORY is to SUBSTANDARD
    (D) DEBILITATE is to DECONSTRUCT
    (E) PROGRESS is to PREVENT

15. BLITHE is to CHEERFUL as
    (A) CALLOUS is to INSENSITIVE
    (B) GARRULOUS is to TACITURN
    (C) IMMUTABLE is to ERRATIC
    (D) OFFICIOUS is to SUPERVISOR
    (E) QUERULOUS is to FAULTFINDER

16. SEAGULL is to FLOCK as WOLF is to
    (A) DEN
    (B) PACK
    (C) CANINE
    (D) PREDATOR
    (E) DEER

17. CACHE is to HOARD as KINDLE is to
    (A) QUENCH
    (B) IGNITE
    (C) CUDDLE
    (D) DOUSE
    (E) HANDLE

18. SINGER is to CHOIR as MUSICIAN is to
    (A) COMPANY
    (B) CAST
    (C) BAND
    (D) INSTRUMENT
    (E) ROCK

19. KNUCKLE is to FINGER as ELBOW is to
    (A) ARM
    (B) SHOULDER
    (C) JOINT
    (D) TORSO
    (E) LEG

20. TABLESPOON is to GALLON as METER is to
    (A) CENTIMETER
    (B) VOLUME
    (C) DISTANCE
    (D) YARD
    (E) KILOMETER

21. QUARTER is to 0.25 as
    (A) NICKEL is to 5.0
    (B) DIME is to 0.1
    (C) PENNY is to 100
    (D) QUINTET is to 5.0
    (E) TRIO is to 3.0

22. KEYBOARD is to COMPUTER as BURNER is to
    (A) KITCHEN
    (B) STOVE
    (C) REFRIGERATOR
    (D) MICROWAVE
    (E) SPATULA

23. HACKNEYED is to ORIGINAL as
    (A) TRITE is to CLICHÉD
    (B) IMAGINATIVE is to CREATIVE
    (C) ECLECTIC is to UNVARIED
    (D) GARBLED is to MUDDLED
    (E) HAPHAZARD is to RANDOM

24. CRUMB is to LOAF as DROP is to
    (A) TIDBIT
    (B) GALLON
    (C) LAZE
    (D) FALL
    (E) FRAGMENT

25. MILE is to DISTANCE as POUND is to
    (A) WEIGHT
    (B) OUNCE
    (C) LENGTH
    (D) HAMMER
    (E) HEADACHE

ARITHMETIC REASONING

This part of the test measures your ability to use arithmetic to solve problems. Each problem is followed by five possible answers. You are to decide which one of the five choices is correct.

1. 85 percent of the senior class at a high school will be graduating. If the class has 540 students, how many students will graduate?

(A) 448
(B) 452
(C) 453
(D) 455
(E) 459

2. In a theater, there are 4,500 lower-level seats and 2,000 upper-level seats. What is the ratio of lower-level seats to total seats?

(A) $\frac{4}{9}$
(B) $\frac{4}{13}$
(C) $\frac{9}{13}$
(D) $\frac{9}{4}$
(E) $\frac{13}{9}$

3. In a class of 20 students, how many conversations must be had so that every student talks to every other student in the class?

(A) 40
(B) 190
(C) 380
(D) 760
(E) 6840

4. Convert 8 pounds, 8 ounces to kilograms to the nearest tenth of a kilogram.

(A) 3.9 kilograms
(B) 4.1 kilograms
(C) 17.6 kilograms
(D) 18.7 kilograms
(E) 19.36 kilograms

5. If an employee who makes $37,500 per year receives a 5.5% raise, what is the employee's new salary?

(A) $35,437.50
(B) $35,625.00
(C) $39,375.00
(D) $39,562.50
(E) $58,125.00

6. Miguel works at a car dealership and is paid a 2 percent commission on every car he sells. If he sells one car for $15,000 and two cars for $12,900 each, how much will he be paid in commissions?

(A) $300
(B) $558
(C) $816
(D) $5,580
(E) $8,160

7. A teacher has 50 notebooks to hand out to students. If she has 16 students in her class, and each student receives 2 notebooks, how many notebooks will she have left over?

(A) 2
(B) 16
(C) 18
(D) 32
(E) 34

8. 40% of what number is equal to 17?

(A) 2.35
(B) 6.8
(C) 42.5
(D) 235
(E) 680

9. During a baseball team's practice, players spent 1 hour at batting practice, 30 minutes catching fly balls, and 15 minutes running sprints. What percentage of the practice did the players spend running sprints?

(A) 14.3

(B) 16.7

(C) 28.6

(D) 33.3

(E) 57.1

10. Michael is making cupcakes. He plans to give $\frac{1}{2}$ of the cupcakes to a friend and $\frac{1}{3}$ of the cupcakes to his coworkers. If he makes 48 cupcakes, how many will he have left over?

(A) 8

(B) 10

(C) 12

(D) 16

(E) 24

11. If the smallest angle in a non-right triangle is 20° and the shortest side is 14, what is the length of the longest side if the largest angle is 100°?

(A) 12.78

(B) 34.31

(C) 40.31

(D) 70.02

(E) 127.81

12. Students board a bus at 7:45 a.m. and arrive at school at 8:20 a.m. How long are the students on the bus?

(A) 30 minutes

(B) 35 minutes

(C) 45 minutes

(D) 50 minutes

(E) 65 minutes

13. Cone A is similar to cone B with a scale factor of 3:4. If the volume of cone A is 54π, what is the volume of cone B?

(A) 72π

(B) 128π

(C) 162π

(D) 216π

(E) 378π

14. An ice chest contains 24 sodas, some regular and some diet. The ratio of diet soda to regular soda is 1:3. How many regular sodas are there in the ice chest?

(A) 1

(B) 4

(C) 6

(D) 18

(E) 24

15. Three people have winning lottery tickets and will split the $500,000 prize between them in a ratio of 3:2:1. How much money will go to the person receiving the most money?

(A) $83,333

(B) $166,666

(C) $250,000

(D) $333,333

(E) $375,000

16. Kim and Chris are writing a book together. Kim wrote twice as many pages as Chris, and together they wrote 240 pages. How many pages did Chris write?

(A) 80

(B) 100

(C) 120

(D) 160

(E) 240

17. If there are 10 millimeters in 1 centimeter, how many millimeters are in 150 centimeters?

(A) 1.5 mm

(B) 15 mm

(C) 150 mm

(D) 1500 mm

(E) 15,000 mm

18. Noah and Jennifer have a total of $10.00 to spend on lunch. If each buys his or her own order of french fries and a soda, how many orders of chicken strips can they share?

Menu

ITEM	PRICE
Hamburger	$4.00
Chicken Strips	$4.00
Onion Rings	$3.00
French Fries	$2.00
Soda	$1.00
Shake	$1.00

(A) 0

(B) 1

(C) 2

(D) 3

(E) 4

19. A store owner purchased 30 refrigerators at a price of $850. He sold them at a 15 percent markup over the price he paid. If he sold all 30 refrigerators, what was his total profit?

(A) $127.50

(B) $977.50

(C) $3,425

(D) $3,825

(E) $4,325

20. Out of 1560 students at Ward Middle School, 15% want to take French. Which expression represents how many students want to take French?

(A) $1560 \div 15$

(B) 1560×15

(C) 1560×0.15

(D) $1560 \div 0.15$

(E) 1560×1.5

21. The number of chairs in the front row of a movie theater is 14. Each subsequent row contains 2 more seats than the row in front of it. If the theater has 25 rows, what is the total number of seats in the theater?

(A) 336

(B) 350

(C) 888

(D) 950

(E) 1014

22. The mean of 13 numbers is 30. The mean of 8 of these numbers is 42. What is the mean of the other 5 numbers?

(A) 5.5

(B) 10.8

(C) 16.4

(D) 21.2

(E) 30.0

23. If a student answers 42 out of 48 questions correctly on a quiz, what percentage of questions did she answer correctly?

(A) 82.5%

(B) 85%

(C) 86%

(D) 87.5%

(E) 90%

24. Robbie has a bag of treats that contains 5 pieces of gum, 7 pieces of taffy, and 8 pieces of chocolate. If Robbie reaches into the bag and randomly pulls out a treat, what is the probability that Robbie will get a piece of taffy?

(A) $\frac{1}{13}$

(B) $\frac{1}{7}$

(C) $\frac{7}{20}$

(D) $\frac{7}{13}$

(E) $\frac{13}{20}$

25. A map is drawn with a scale of 1 inch = 25 miles. If two cities are 115 miles apart, how far apart will they be on the map?

(A) 2.6 inches

(B) 2.9 inches

(C) 3.2 inches

(D) 4.6 inches

(E) 4.9 inches

WORD KNOWLEDGE

This part of the test measures your knowledge of words and their meanings. For each question, you are to choose the word below that is closest in meaning to the capitalized word above.

1. SUBSTANTIAL
   (A) partial
   (B) inferior
   (C) plentiful
   (D) upright
   (E) chunky

2. ACRIMONIOUS
   (A) bitter
   (B) inedible
   (C) smoky
   (D) rotten
   (E) loud

3. INCLEMENT
   (A) hostile
   (B) sparse
   (C) stormy
   (D) distressing
   (E) dehydrated

4. CONCILIATORY
   (A) wise
   (B) tender
   (C) moderate
   (D) peacemaking
   (E) pharmaceutical

5. TACITURN
   (A) aloof
   (B) penniless
   (C) agreeable
   (D) changeable
   (E) jagged

6. CONCURRENT
   (A) up to date
   (B) surging
   (C) splashy
   (D) sophisticated
   (E) simultaneous

7. ELUSIVE
   (A) mysterious
   (B) underhanded
   (C) slimy
   (D) snakelike
   (E) nonsensical

8. COMPLICITY
   (A) self-satisfaction
   (B) creation—often of an artwork
   (C) participation—often in a crime
   (D) straightforwardness
   (E) exactitude

9. RELEGATE
   (A) assign
   (B) demote
   (C) survey
   (D) distribute
   (E) communicate

10. MONOLITHIC
    (A) single-minded
    (B) intimidating
    (C) colossal
    (D) stony
    (E) alone

11. LAMPOON
    (A) pierce
    (B) capture
    (C) ridicule
    (D) cheer
    (E) persuade

12. PATRIARCH
    (A) patriotic person
    (B) gentle leader
    (C) huge doorway
    (D) head man
    (E) mother figure

13. SENSORY
    (A) weather-related
    (B) regretful
    (C) faith-based
    (D) critical
    (E) physical

14. QUALITATIVE
    (A) licensed
    (B) unfamiliar
    (C) pleasurable
    (D) based on size, number, or amount
    (E) based on good and bad characteristics

15. OBSEQUIOUS
    (A) apparent
    (B) ignorant
    (C) submissive
    (D) repressive
    (E) despicable

16. NOXIOUS
    (A) unfriendly
    (B) poisonous
    (C) irritating
    (D) smooth
    (E) nauseated

17. MISANTHROPIC
    (A) having a fear of spiders
    (B) calm and philosophical
    (C) having a fear of flying
    (D) distrustful and reclusive
    (E) naïve and open to new ideas

18. FELICITY
    (A) catlike
    (B) emotion
    (C) disorder
    (D) irrelevance
    (E) contentment

19. CHIVALROUS
    (A) warlike
    (B) courteous
    (C) hounded
    (D) cowardly
    (E) quivering

20. EXPROPRIATE
    (A) steal it
    (B) leave it
    (C) collect it
    (D) buy it
    (E) repair it

21. EBB
    (A) drift
    (B) network
    (C) motivate
    (D) recede
    (E) waddle

22. ICONOCLAST
    (A) symbol
    (B) rebel
    (C) fastener
    (D) inference
    (E) warning

23. PRAGMATIC
    (A) accurate
    (B) tedious
    (C) realistic
    (D) imaginative
    (E) impulsive

24. CACOPHONY
    (A) harsh sound
    (B) melodious music
    (C) synthetic product
    (D) artificial flavor
    (E) sweet taste

25. CAJOLE
    (A) persuade
    (B) cheer up
    (C) imprison
    (D) compel
    (E) revolve

MATH KNOWLEDGE

This part of the test measures your knowledge of mathematical terms and principles. Each problem is followed by five possible answers. You are to decide which one of the five choices is correct.

1. A cube is inscribed in a sphere such that each vertex on the cube touches the sphere. If the volume of the sphere is 972π cm^3, what is the approximate volume of the cube in cubic centimeters?

(A) 9

(B) 104

(C) 927

(D) 1125

(E) 1729

2. $\frac{7}{8} - \frac{1}{10} - \frac{2}{3}$

(A) $\frac{1}{30}$

(B) $\frac{4}{120}$

(C) $\frac{13}{120}$

(D) $\frac{4}{21}$

(E) $\frac{4}{105}$

3. If $j = 4$, what is the value of $2(j-4)^4 - j + \frac{1}{2}j$?

(A) 0

(B) −2

(C) 2

(D) 4

(E) 32

4. Solve for y: $3y + 2x = 15z$

(A) $y = \frac{3}{15z} - 2x$

(B) $y = \frac{-2x + 15z}{3}$

(C) $y = -\frac{2}{3}x + 15z$

(D) $y = -2x + 5z$

(E) $y = \frac{3}{2x - 15z}$

5. Which of the following is equivalent to $54z^4 + 18z^3 + 3z + 3$?

(A) $18z^4 + 6z^3 + z + 1$

(B) $3z(18z^3 + 6z^2 + 1)$

(C) $3(18z^4 + 6z^3 + z + 1)$

(D) $72z^7 + 3z$

(E) $54(z^4 + 18z^3 + 3z + 3)$

6. What is the area of the shape?

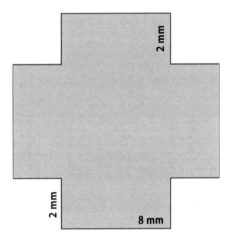

(A) 6 mm^2

(B) 16 mm^2

(C) 64 mm^2

(D) 128 mm^2

(E) 144 mm^2

7. 50 shares of a financial stock and 10 shares of an auto stock are valued at $1,300. If 10 shares of the financial stock and 10 shares of the auto stock are valued at $500, what is the value of 50 shares of the auto stock?

(A) $30

(B) $20

(C) $1,300

(D) $1,500

(E) $1,800

8. Solve for x: $4x + 12 = x - 3$

(A) $x = -5$

(B) $x = -3$

(C) $x = 1.8$

(D) $x = 5$

(E) $x = 15$

9. Simplify: $\left(\dfrac{4x^{-3}y^4z}{8x^{-5}y^3z^{-2}}\right)^2$

(A) $\dfrac{x^4yz^3}{2}$

(B) $\dfrac{x^4y^2z^6}{2}$

(C) $\dfrac{x^4y^2z^6}{4}$

(D) $\dfrac{x^4yz^3}{4}$

(E) $\dfrac{x^4y^2z^6}{8}$

10. Two spheres are tangent to each other. One has a volume of 36π, and the other has a volume of 288π. What is the greatest distance between a point on one of the spheres and a point on the other sphere?

(A) 6

(B) 9

(C) 18

(D) 36

(E) 63

11. Factor $4a^3b + 10ab^2$

(A) $ab(4a^2 + 5b^2)$

(B) $ab(a^2b + 10b)$

(C) $2ab(2a^2 + 5b)$

(D) $2a^2b(2ab + 5)$

(E) $4a^2b(a + 5b)$

12. What is 498,235 rounded to the nearest thousands?

(A) 498,000

(B) 498,200

(C) 499,000

(D) 499,200

(E) 500,000

13. Which of the following is the y-intercept of the given equation?
$7y - 42x + 7 = 0$

(A) $(0, \frac{1}{6})$

(B) $(6, 0)$

(C) $(0, -1)$

(D) $(-1, 0)$

(E) $(0, 7)$

14. The value $(3 + \sqrt{2})(3 - \sqrt{2})$ is equal to

(A) 7

(B) 9

(C) 13

(D) $9 - 2\sqrt{2}$

(E) $7 + 6\sqrt{2}$

15. A wedge from a cylindrical piece of cheese was cut as shown. If the entire wheel of cheese weighed 73 pounds before the wedge was removed, what is the approximate remaining weight of the cheese?

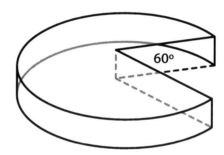

(A) 12.17 pounds

(B) 37.00 pounds

(C) 55.00 pounds

(D) 60.83 pounds

(E) 66.92 pounds

16. Which of the following is a solution to the inequality $2x + y \le -10$?

(A) $(0, 0)$

(B) $(10, 2)$

(C) $(10, 10)$

(D) $(-10, -10)$

(E) $(0, 10)$

17. Solve for x.

$x = 6(3^0)$

(A) 0

(B) 1

(C) 6

(D) 18

(E) 180

18. The sum of the internal angles of a quadrilateral is

(A) 90°

(B) 180°

(C) 270°

(D) 360°

(E) 540°

19. $(3x + 2)^2 =$

(A) $9x^2 + 4$

(B) $9x^2 + 36$

(C) $9x^2 + 6x + 4$

(D) $9x^2 + 10x + 4$

(E) $9x^2 + 12x + 4$

20. If the volume of a cube is 343 cubic meters, what is the cube's surface area?

(A) 49 m^2

(B) 84 m^2

(C) 196 m^2

(D) 294 m^2

(E) 343 m^2

21. What is the distance on the x,y-coordinate plane between the points $(3, 0)$ and $(-2, -5)$?

(A) $\sqrt{6}$

(B) $\sqrt{10}$

(C) $\sqrt{29}$

(D) $5\sqrt{2}$

(E) $10\sqrt{5}$

22. What is the value of $3x + 7y - 4$ if $x = 8$ and $y = 2$?

(A) 34

(B) 38

(C) 42

(D) 58

(E) 62

23. If one leg of a right triangle has a length of 40, which of the following could be the lengths of the two remaining sides?

(A) 50 and 41

(B) 9 and 41

(C) 9 and 30

(D) 50 and 63

(E) 41 and 63

24. The formula for distance is $d = v \times t$, where v is the object's velocity and t is the time. How long will it take a plane to fly 4000 miles from Chicago to London if the plane flies at a constant rate of 500 mph?

(A) 0.125 hours

(B) 3.5 hours

(C) 8 hours

(D) 20 hours

(E) 45 hours

25. Multiply the terms $3x^2yz^4$ and $6xy^3z^2$.

(A) $9x^2y^3z^8$

(B) $9x^3y^4z^6$

(C) $18xy^2z^2$

(D) $18x^2y^3z^8$

(E) $18x^3y^4z^6$

READING COMPREHENSION

This part of the test measures your ability to read and understand written material. Each passage is followed by a series of multiple-choice questions. You are to choose the option that best answers the question based on the passage. No additional information or specific knowledge is needed.

The Vietnam War is known for the introduction of controversial and harmful weaponry, like Agent Orange and napalm, which were later discontinued by the US military. However, the conflict also marked the emergence of a mainstay of current American military operations: the helicopter. Although the first operational helicopter took flight in 1939, with the first military helicopter following shortly after in 1942, it was not until the Vietnam War that the military began to rely on helicopters both as transport tools and offensive weapons.

The first American military use of helicopters was very specific and targeted American bombers that had crash-landed in Burma while flying supplies to Chiang Kai-Shek's forces in China. The military first attempted to use silent gliders to recover the troops, but they could not access the remote mountain area. So, they turned to the new helicopter. Because they did not need long landing strips, helicopters were able to navigate the treacherous mountains and extract the flight crews. This success bolstered American military interest in helicopters and led to investment in building US supply. As a result, during the Korean War, use of helicopters expanded from extraction of downed crews to medical evacuations. Helicopters still, however, had no role in direct combat.

When the Vietnam War began, the United States expected it to progress in the same manner as the preceding wars. Vietnam, a small country, had little military experience or might. Helicopter use was incorporated into planning, but only as it had been conventionally used: for extraction and evacuation. Military experts expected a quick war that would showcase the superiority of conventional American weapons, not a war that would spur innovation.

However, the North Vietnamese Viet Cong were preparing for a very different war than the Americans. The Viet Cong modeled their military strategy after Mao Zedong's successful guerilla movement in China. As the United States established air bases and headquarters, the Viet Cong infiltrated the jungles and its villages by blending in with the local population and winning their allegiance. American troops found themselves marching for days without encountering an enemy, while others were ambushed and caught unawares. The United States faced a new military challenge: How to defeat an enemy that avoided confrontation? Rather than focusing efforts on building complex military infrastructure, US strategy shifted to finding ways to draw the Viet Cong out. The most successful strategy was to insert American troops across enemy lines. However, that meant transporting troops quickly into mountainous jungle territory. For that, American troops in Vietnam needed helicopters.

Helicopters like the CH-47, also called the Chinook, and the Huey could carry large numbers of troops and land in small clearings in the jungle. As a result, helicopters quickly became one of the primary military tools of the war, and—in spite of all intentions—American military strategy began to transform. These helicopters often faced fire as they crossed into enemy territory, so crew members began to carry rifles to shoot at combatants in defense. To increase defense capabilities and efficiency, crews began mounting heavy weaponry onto their helicopters, creating the first helicopter gunships. Eventually, Gatling guns, or mini-guns, were mounted onto most helicopters. Because of the increased importance, of these guns, military research focused on improving and refining them until they could fire thousands of rounds per minute.

While increased use of the helicopter and the innovations that came with it did not garner a win for the United States in Vietnam, it did alter American military resources and strategy going forward. Inserting troops across enemy lines using helicopters, a tactic now known as an air assault, was adopted in Afghanistan, whose mountainous terrain recalled that of Vietnam, and whose combatants used similar guerilla tactics. Attack helicopters are also now a staple of the US military, used most recently to provide air support to ground troops in conflicts in Afghanistan and Iraq. They can be called up faster than jets and can hover longer. They are still the preferred tools for extraction of stranded crew and troops and for the evacuation of injured soldiers. The versatility of helicopters has made them one of the most valued assets in the modern military.

1. The main idea of the passage is that
   (A) the Vietnam War required the US military to develop a new military strategy.
   (B) although developed in World War II, armed helicopters were not used until the Vietnam War.
   (C) in Vietnam, the United States discovered that mountainous areas are very challenging in military combat.
   (D) the Vietnam War increased the importance of helicopters to the US military.
   (E) currently, the US military uses helicopters primarily for evacuation and extraction.

2. Which of the following is NOT a fact stated in the passage?
   (A) The Viet Cong based their military strategy after the tactics of Chinese rebels.
   (B) Helicopters were the only transport successful at extracting downed crews in Burma.
   (C) Viet Cong fighters evaded direct combat with American troops.
   (D) The arming of military helicopters began as a self-defense tactic.
   (E) The number of helicopters in the US military did not increase much from World War II to the Korean War.

3. Which of the following is a statement of fact from the passage?
   (A) The United States had the military advantage over the Viet Cong.
   (B) Air assaults emerged as a military tactic after the Vietnam War.
   (C) The use of helicopters for medical evacuation developed during the Korean War.
   (D) Helicopters were used to support other weaponry like Agent Orange and napalm.
   (E) The Viet Cong focused on military infrastructure and weaponry at the beginning of the war.

4. It can be inferred from the passage that
   (A) the United States developed an informed military plan before entering the war in Vietnam.
   (B) American military practices in World War II and the Korean War were unhelpful to American troops in Vietnam.
   (C) helicopters are most useful in jungle conditions similar to that of Vietnam.
   (D) helicopters are currently the primary combat tool used by the American military.
   (E) the Viet Cong adopted the American practice of using helicopters as military tools.

5. In the fourth paragraph, the world *infiltrated* most nearly means
   (A) entered gradually.
   (B) intensely suffered.
   (C) rapidly migrated.
   (D) successfully avoided.
   (E) controlled completely.

6. With which of the following claims about American military use of helicopters would the author most likely agree?
   (A) Helicopters will play an important role in US military strategy for years to come.
   (B) The US military has become overdependent on helicopters in the past four decades.
   (C) The use of helicopters in combat has greatly reduced the loss of life among American troops.
   (D) American investment in helicopters should be reinvested into other military weapons and tools.
   (E) The arming of helicopters was an unnecessary and unprofitable development in military strategy.

Excerpted from "Introduction," Worldwide Effects of Nuclear War: Some Perspectives, United States Arms Control and Disarmament Agency

It has now been two decades since the introduction of thermonuclear fusion weapons into the military inventories of the great powers, and more than a decade since the United States, Great Britain, and the Soviet Union ceased to test nuclear weapons in the atmosphere. Today our understanding of the technology of thermonuclear weapons seems highly advanced, but our knowledge of the physical and biological consequences of nuclear war is continuously evolving.

Only recently, new light was shed on the subject in a study which the Arms Control and Disarmament Agency had asked the National Academy of Sciences to undertake. Previous studies had tended to focus very largely on radioactive fallout from a nuclear war; an important aspect of this new study was its inquiry into all possible consequences, including the effects of large-scale nuclear detonations on the ozone layer which helps protect life on earth from the sun's ultraviolet radiations. Assuming a total detonation of 10,000 megatons—a large-scale but less than total nuclear "exchange," as one would say in the dehumanizing jargon of the strategists—it was concluded that as much as 30–70 percent of the ozone might be eliminated from the northern hemisphere (where a nuclear war would presumably take place) and as much as 20–40 percent from the southern hemisphere. Recovery would probably take about 3–10 years, but the Academy's study notes that long term global changes cannot be completely ruled out.

The reduced ozone concentrations would have a number of consequences outside the areas in which the detonations occurred. The Academy study notes, for example, that the resultant increase in ultraviolet would cause "prompt incapacitating cases of sunburn in the temperate zones and snow blindness in northern countries . . ."

Strange though it might seem, the increased ultraviolet radiation could also be accompanied by a drop in the average temperature. The size of the change is open to question, but the largest changes would probably occur at the higher latitudes, where crop production and ecological balances are sensitively dependent on the number of frost-free days and other factors related to average temperature. The Academy's study concluded that ozone changes due to nuclear war might decrease global surface temperatures by only negligible amounts or by as much as a few degrees. To calibrate the significance of this, the study mentioned that a cooling of even 1 degree centigrade would eliminate commercial wheat growing in Canada.

Thus, the possibility of a serious increase in ultraviolet radiation has been added to widespread radioactive fallout as a fearsome consequence of the large-scale use of nuclear weapons. And it is likely that we must reckon with still other complex and subtle processes, global in scope, which could seriously threaten the health of distant populations in the event of an all-out nuclear war.

Up to now, many of the important discoveries about nuclear weapon effects have been made not through deliberate scientific inquiry but by accident. And as the following historical examples show, there has been a series of surprises.

"Castle/Bravo" was the largest nuclear weapon ever detonated by the United States. Before it was set off at Bikini on February 28, 1954, it was expected to explode with an energy equivalent of about 8 million tons of TNT. Actually, it produced almost twice that explosive power—equivalent to 15 million tons of TNT.

If the power of the bomb was unexpected, so were the after-effects. About 6 hours after the explosion, a fine, sandy ash began to sprinkle the Japanese fishing vessel Lucky Dragon, some 90 miles downwind of the burst point, and Rongelap Atoll, 100 miles downwind. Though 40 to 50 miles away from the proscribed test area, the vessel's crew and the islanders received heavy doses of radiation from the weapon's "fallout"—the coral rock, soil, and other debris sucked up in the fireball and made intensively radioactive by the nuclear reaction. One radioactive isotope in the fallout, iodine-131, rapidly built up to serious concentration in the thyroid glands of the victims, particularly young Rongelapese children.

More than any other event in the decade of testing large nuclear weapons in the atmosphere, Castle/Bravo's unexpected contamination of 7,000 square miles of the Pacific Ocean dramatically illustrated how large-scale nuclear war could produce casualties on a colossal scale, far beyond the local effects of blast and fire alone.

7. The primary purpose of the passage is to
   (A) describe the effects of large-scale detonations on the ozone layer.
   (B) compare an increase in ultraviolet radiation to an increase in radioactive fallout.
   (C) explain the aftereffects of the 1954 nuclear blast.
   (D) provide facts about the consequences of a nuclear war.
   (E) emphasize the damage created by the testing of nuclear weapons.

8. The author would most likely recommend that
   (A) information about the consequences of using nuclear weapons be spread to all countries.
   (B) Americans stop producing nuclear weapons.
   (C) all countries stop testing nuclear weapons.
   (D) research continue on the historical examples of nuclear power.
   (E) the aftereffects of the production of nuclear weapons be published, in all languages.

9. In the second paragraph, the term *dehumanizing jargon* refers to
    (A) detonation of 10,000 megatons
    (B) nuclear "exchange"
    (C) large-scale detonation
    (D) study of the Arms Control and Disarmament Agency
    (E) ultraviolent radiation

10. The author's attitude toward the past and potential use of nuclear weapons is best described as one of
    (A) indifference.
    (B) urgency.
    (C) bewilderment.
    (D) despair.
    (E) ambivalence.

11. Which of the following best describes the organization of the passage?
    (A) The problem of nuclear detonations and war is discussed; then, possible solutions are evaluated.
    (B) The term thermonuclear technology is defined with scientific explanations.
    (C) Explanations are provided of each of the advances in knowledge of nuclear war.
    (D) Descriptions are included of each nuclear detonation that occurred in the twentieth century.
    (E) Research is explained with a series of results from scientific studies.

12. The author notes that "Castle/Bravo" was the largest nuclear weapon ever detonated by the United States in order to identify the
    (A) unexpected power and after-effects of a detonated nuclear weapon.
    (B) flaw in the view that nuclear weapons are sometimes necessary.
    (C) issue that led to the ban on nuclear weapons.
    (D) perspective that accidents are associated with nuclear material.
    (E) controversy over the significance of the detonation.

13. According to the passage, why do scientists believe that long-term global changes are a possible consequence of nuclear war?
    (A) Recovery from nuclear detonation takes a long time.
    (B) The northern hemisphere would be eliminated.
    (C) The ozone layer would be damaged and ultraviolet radiation would increase.
    (D) Widespread ecological imbalances would create panic.
    (E) The people of the southern hemisphere would be forced to migrate.

Adapted from an address given by Harry S. Truman before a joint session of Congress in 1947.

One of the primary objectives of the foreign policy of the United States is the creation of conditions in which we and other nations will be able to work out a way of life free from coercion. This was a fundamental issue in the war with Germany and Japan. Our victory was won over countries which sought to impose their will, and their way of life, upon other nations.

To ensure the peaceful development of nations, free from coercion, the United States has taken a leading part in establishing the United Nations. The United Nations is designed to make possible lasting freedom and independence for all its members. We shall not realize our objectives, however, unless we are willing to help free peoples to maintain their free institutions and their national integrity against aggressive movements that seek to impose upon them totalitarian regimes. This is no more than a frank recognition that totalitarian regimes imposed on free peoples, by direct or indirect aggression, undermine the foundations of international peace and hence the security of the United States.

The peoples of a number of countries of the world have recently had totalitarian regimes forced upon them against their will. The Government of the United States has made frequent protests against coercion and intimidation, in violation of the Yalta agreement, in Poland, Romania, and Bulgaria. I must also state that in a number of other countries there have been similar developments.

At the present moment in world history nearly every nation must choose between alternative ways of life. The choice is too often not a free one.

One way of life is based upon the will of the majority, and is distinguished by free institutions, representative government, free elections, guarantees of individual liberty, freedom of speech and religion, and freedom from political oppression.

The second way of life is based upon the will of a minority forcibly imposed upon the majority. It relies upon terror and oppression, a controlled press and radio; fixed elections, and the suppression of personal freedoms.

I believe that it must be the policy of the United States to support free peoples who are resisting attempted subjugation by armed minorities or by outside pressures.

I believe that we must assist free peoples to work out their own destinies in their own way.

14. As used in the first paragraph, *coercion* most nearly means
   (A) intimidation
   (B) brutality
   (C) cruelty
   (D) authority
   (E) anger

15. President Truman most likely references the war with Germany and Japan in order to
   (A) remind Americans of the nation's stance on foreign intervention.
   (B) reassure Americans that they can win another war.
   (C) suggest a comparison between the current situation and the one that led to the Second World War.
   (D) distinguish between the current situation and the one that led to America's intervention in the war.
   (E) create apprehension about America's future.

16. In the fifth and sixth paragraphs, Truman most likely contrasts two ways of life in order to

(A) illustrate some of the benefits of a democratic government.

(B) challenge the tyrannical leaders of oppressed nations to reconsider their approach to government.

(C) describe the reasons that America might consider intervening in a foreign nation.

(D) suggest that free people have a responsibility to fight on behalf of those who are not free.

(E) create fear around the possible loss of freedom that Americans might experience if totalitarian regimes are allowed to prosper.

Influenza (also called the flu) has historically been one of the most common, and deadliest, human infections. While many people who contract the virus will recover, many others will not. Over the past 150 years, tens of millions of people have died from the flu, and millions more have been left with lingering complications such as secondary infections.

Although it's a common disease, the flu is not actually highly infectious, meaning it's relatively difficult to contract. The flu can only be transmitted when individuals come into direct contact with bodily fluids of people infected with the flu or when they are exposed to expelled aerosol particles (which result from coughing and sneezing). Because the viruses can only travel short distances as aerosol particles and will die within a few hours on hard surfaces, the virus can be contained with fairly simple health measures like hand washing and face masks.

However, the spread of the flu can only be contained when people are aware such measures need to be taken. One of the reasons the flu has historically been so deadly is the amount of time between when people become infectious and when they develop symptoms. Viral shedding—the process by which the body releases viruses that have been successfully reproducing during the infection—takes place two days after infection, while symptoms do not usually develop until the third day of infection. Thus, infected individuals have at least twenty-four hours in which they may unknowingly infect others.

17. The main idea of the passage is that

(A) the flu is a deadly disease that's difficult to control because people become infectious before they show symptoms.

(B) for the flu to be transmitted, individuals must come in contact with bodily fluids from infected individuals.

(C) the spread of the flu is easy to contain because the viruses do not live long either as aerosol particles or on hard surfaces.

(D) the flu has killed tens of millions of people and can often cause deadly secondary infections.

(E) influenza is not as highly infectious as people assume it to be.

18. According to the passage, which of the following correctly describes the flu?

(A) The flu is easy to contract and always fatal.

(B) The flu is difficult to contract and always fatal.

(C) The flu is easy to contract and sometimes fatal.

(D) The flu is difficult to contract and sometimes fatal.

(E) The flu is easy to contract but rarely fatal.

19. According to the passage, why is the flu considered to not be highly infectious?

   (A) Many people who get the flu will recover and have no lasting complications, so only a small number of people who become infected will die.

   (B) The process of viral shedding takes two days, so infected individuals have enough time to implement simple health measures that stop the spread of the disease.

   (C) The flu virus cannot travel far or live for long periods of time outside the human body, so its spread can easily be contained.

   (D) Twenty-four hours is a relatively short period of time for the virus to spread among a population.

   (E) Most people who become infected never show symptoms.

20. In the last paragraph, the word *measures* most nearly means

   (A) a plan of action

   (B) a standard unit

   (C) an adequate amount

   (D) a rhythmic movement

   (E) a known quantity

21. Which statement is NOT a detail from the passage?

   (A) Tens of millions of people have been killed by the flu virus.

   (B) There is typically a twenty-four hour window during which individuals are infectious but not showing flu symptoms.

   (C) Viral shedding is the process by which people recover from the flu.

   (D) The flu can be transmitted by direct contact with bodily fluids from infected individuals or by exposure to aerosol particles.

   (E) The virus can travel only short distances in the air and survives only a few hours on hard surfaces.

22. Which of the following can be inferred from the passage?

   (A) Preemptively implementing health measures like hand washing and face masks could help stop the spread of the flu virus.

   (B) Doctors are not sure how the flu virus is transmitted, so they are unsure how to stop it from spreading.

   (C) The flu is dangerous because it is both deadly and highly infectious.

   (D) Individuals stop being infectious three days after they are infected.

   (E) The flu virus is not something to worry about, as it is not very highly infectious.

In its most basic form, geography is the study of space; more specifically, it studies the physical space of the earth and the ways in which it interacts with, shapes, and is shaped by its habitants. Geographers look at the world from a spatial perspective. This means that at the center of all geographic study is the question, *where?* For geographers, the *where* of any interaction, event, or development is a crucial element to understanding it.

This question of *where* can be asked in a variety of fields of study, so there are many sub-disciplines of geography. These can be organized into four main categories: 1) regional studies, which examine the characteristics of a particular place; 2) topical studies, which look at a single physical or human feature that impacts the whole world; 3) physical studies, which focus on the physical features of Earth; and 4) human studies, which examine the relationship between human activity and the environment.

23.   A researcher studying the relationship between farming and river systems would be engaged in which of the following geographical sub-disciplines?

(A) regional studies

(B) topical studies

(C) physical studies

(D) human studies

(E) physical and human studies

24.   Which of the following best describes the purpose of the passage?

(A) expository

(B) narrative

(C) persuasive

(D) descriptive

(E) rhetorical

25.   Which of the following is a concise summary of the passage?

(A) The most important questions in geography are where an event or development took place.

(B) Geography, which is the study of the physical space on Earth, can be broken down into four sub-disciplines.

(C) Regional studies is the study of a single region or area.

(D) Geography can be broken down into four sub-disciplines: regional studies, topical studies, physical studies, and human studies.

(E) The relationship between humans and their physical space is an important one.

PHYSICAL SCIENCE

This part of the test measures your knowledge in the area of science. Each of the questions or incomplete statements is followed by five choices. You are to decide which one of the choices best answers the question or completes the statement.

1. Energy is the capacity of an object to do work and is measured in
   (A) joules.
   (B) watts.
   (C) newtons.
   (D) meters.
   (E) hertz.

2. What is the name of the phenomenon when a star suddenly increases in brightness and then disappears from view?
   (A) aurora
   (B) galaxy
   (C) black hole
   (D) eclipse
   (E) supernova

3. Which measurement describes the distance between crests in a wave?
   (A) amplitude
   (B) wavelength
   (C) frequency
   (D) period
   (E) pitch

4. Which of the following is a heterogeneous mixture?
   (A) soil
   (B) salt water
   (C) steel
   (D) air
   (E) vinegar

5. Which planet does NOT have a moon?
   (A) Mercury
   (B) Earth
   (C) Jupiter
   (D) Saturn
   (E) Venus

6. Which substance is a good thermal conductor?
   (A) plastic
   (B) rubber
   (C) porcelain
   (D) air
   (E) aluminum

7. Which process allows the transfer of heat to occur from the contact between two substances?
   (A) conduction
   (B) convection
   (C) radiation
   (D) sublimation
   (E) evaporation

8. Two negative charges are held at a distance of 1 m from each other. When the charges are released, they will
   (A) remain at rest.
   (B) move closer together.
   (C) move farther apart.
   (D) move together in the same direction.
   (E) move separately in random directions.

9. Which of the following correctly describes a strong acid?

   (A) A strong acid completely ionizes in water.

   (B) A strong acid donates more than one proton.

   (C) A strong acid has a pH close to 7.

   (D) A strong acid will not ionize.

   (E) A strong acid contains at least one metal atom.

10. What are the negatively charged particles inside an atom?

    (A) protons

    (B) neutrons

    (C) electrons

    (D) ions

    (E) nucleus

11. Which characteristic generally increases as altitude increases in the troposphere?

    (A) temperature

    (B) pressure

    (C) density

    (D) all of the above

    (E) none of the above

12. Which type of cloud is associated with fair weather and is composed entirely of ice crystals?

    (A) stratus

    (B) cumulonimbus

    (C) cirrus

    (D) nimbostratus

    (E) stratocumulus

13. Which statement about mass and weight is true?

    (A) Mass and weight always have the same value.

    (B) Mass is created by gravitational pull.

    (C) Weight is created by gravitational pull.

    (D) Mass is related to the surface area of an object.

    (E) Weight is unaffected by location.

14. Which process within the rock cycle creates metamorphic rock?

    (A) compaction

    (B) heat and pressure

    (C) crystallization

    (D) weathering

    (E) erosion

15. Which tool is used to measure the mass of an object?

    (A) thermometer

    (B) graduated cylinder

    (C) balance

    (D) ammeter

    (E) ruler

16. Which action is an example of mechanical weathering?

    (A) Calcium carbonate reacts with water to form a cave.

    (B) An iron gate rusts.

    (C) Tree roots grow under the foundation of a house and cause cracks.

    (D) Bananas turn brown after they are peeled.

    (E) Feldspar turns to clay when exposed to water.

17. Which pH level is classified as a base?

    (A) 1
    (B) 4
    (C) 6
    (D) 7
    (E) 8

18. What is the term for the top layer of the earth's surface?

    (A) exosphere
    (B) lithosphere
    (C) atmosphere
    (D) biosphere
    (E) asthenosphere

19. Valence electrons are important in a circuit because they

    (A) can easily change between positive and negative charge.
    (B) allow protons to flow through the circuit, creating current.
    (C) are stored in the circuit's voltage source.
    (D) carry the charge in conducting materials.
    (E) form the chemical bonds necessary to carry current.

20. Which energy source is nonrenewable?

    (A) water
    (B) wind
    (C) coal
    (D) sunlight
    (E) geothermal

TABLE READING

This part of the test measures your ability to read a table quickly and accurately. Your task will be to find the block where the column and row intersect, note the number that appears there, and then find this number among the five answer options.

		x-value					
		0	**2**	**4**	**6**	**8**	**10**
	1	35	35	35	37	37	37
	2	37	39	40	42	42	42
y-value	**3**	40	42	45	45	46	46
	4	43	46	46	48	49	51
	5	46	49	51	51	51	53

	x	y	(A)	(B)	(C)	(D)	(E)
1.	4	2	35	40	42	45	51
2.	8	4	35	37	42	49	51
3.	6	5	37	40	46	49	51
4.	10	2	40	42	45	49	51
5.	2	3	37	42	46	49	51

Comparison of Distance

INCHES	FEET	METERS
5	0.417	0.127
10	0.83	0.254
15	1.25	0.381
20	1.67	0.508
25	2.08	0.635
30	2.5	0.762

6. How many inches equal 0.381 meters?

(A) 0.417

(B) 0.508

(C) 5

(D) 10

(E) 15

7. How many meters is 2.5 feet?

(A) 0.127

(B) 0.508

(C) 0.762

(D) 2.08

(E) 2.5

8. How many feet equates to 15 inches?

(A) 0.254
(B) 0.83
(C) 1
(D) 1.25
(E) 1.50

9. How many feet are in 0.508 meters?

(A) 1.25
(B) 1.67
(C) 2.08
(D) 2.54
(E) 20

10. How many inches are in 0.254 meters?

(A) 0.83
(B) 10
(C) 15
(D) 20
(E) 25

Basic Allowance for Housing (BAH)—Ft. Campbell, KY

| | | 2016 | | 2017 | |
		With Dependents	Without Dependents	With Dependents	Without Dependents
RANK	O-1	1,437	1,278	1,317	1,197
	O-2	1,536	1,398	1,377	1,290
	O-3	1,647	1,494	1,788	1,389
	O-4	1,902	1,575	1,962	1,545
	O-5	2,088	1,599	2,085	1,641

11. What is the 2017 BAH for an O-3 with dependents?

(A) 1,317
(B) 1,494
(C) 1,647
(D) 1,788
(E) 1,902

12. How much did the 2017 BAH for an O-2 without dependents decrease from 2016?

(A) 85
(B) 90
(C) 92
(D) 108
(E) 110

13. What was the 2016 BAH for an O-4 without dependents?

(A) 1,494
(B) 1,545
(C) 1,575
(D) 1,902
(E) 1,962

14. What is the difference of the 2017 BAH for an O-2 with dependents and an O-3 with dependents?

(A) 60
(B) 81
(C) 99
(D) 111
(E) 411

15. What is the difference in the 2017 BAH for an O-2 with and without dependents?

    (A) 54
    (B) 64
    (C) 87
    (D) 138
    (E) 203

Name and Information

NAME	OCCUPATION	AGE (YEARS)
Ann	Cashier	20
Barb	Dealer	22
Don	Engineer	26
Edward	Owner	36
George	Student	37
John	Teacher	39
Kristin	Tutor	42
Michelle	Veterinarian	45

16. Who is thirty-nine years old?

    (A) Ann
    (B) the dealer
    (C) the engineer
    (D) John
    (E) the veterinarian

17. What is the age of the engineer?

    (A) twenty
    (B) five
    (C) twenty-six
    (D) thirty-six
    (E) forty-five

18. What is Kristin's occupation?

    (A) engineer
    (B) George
    (C) forty-two
    (D) teacher
    (E) tutor

19. What is George's age?

    (A) thirty-six
    (B) twenty-two
    (C) thirty-seven
    (D) forty-five
    (E) thirty-nine

20. Who listed is a veterinarian?

    (A) Ann
    (B) Edward
    (C) John
    (D) Kristin
    (E) Michelle

Weight Comparison (Imperial)

QUART	PINT	GALLON
$\frac{1}{2}$	1	0.125
1	2	$\frac{1}{4}$
4	8	1
8	16	2
12	24	3
16	32	4

21. How many pints are in 1 gallon?

(A) 2

(B) 4

(C) 8

(D) 12

(E) 16

24. How many quarts are in 3 gallons?

(A) 10

(B) 12

(C) 16

(D) 20

(E) 25

22. If one quart is 32 ounces, how many ounces are in 1 gallon?

(A) 64

(B) 96

(C) 115

(D) 128

(E) 256

25. A pint is 16 ounces. How many ounces are in 1 quart?

(A) 8

(B) 16

(C) 25

(D) 30

(E) 32

23. How many pints are in 1 quart?

(A) 2

(B) 3

(C) 4

(D) 5

(E) 6

Sample Recipe

SERVINGS	FLOUR (CUPS)	SUGAR (CUPS)	MILK (CUPS)	EGGS
8	1 and $\frac{1}{4}$	$\frac{1}{4}$	$\frac{1}{3}$	1
10	1 and $\frac{1}{2}$	$\frac{1}{2}$	$\frac{2}{3}$	2
12	1 and $\frac{3}{4}$	$\frac{3}{4}$	1 and $\frac{1}{3}$	3
16	2 and $\frac{1}{4}$	1	1 and $\frac{2}{3}$	4

26. How much sugar is needed when three eggs are used?

(A) $\frac{1}{4}$

(B) $\frac{3}{4}$

(C) 1

(D) 1 and $\frac{3}{4}$

(E) 1 and $\frac{1}{3}$

27. How much flour is needed if 1 and $\frac{1}{3}$ cups of milk are used?

(A) 1

(B) 1 and $\frac{3}{4}$

(C) 2 and $\frac{1}{4}$

(D) 2 and $\frac{1}{2}$

(E) 3

28. How many servings are made when three eggs are used?

(A) 3

(B) 4

(C) 8

(D) 12

(E) 16

29. How much milk is needed to make eight servings?

(A) $\frac{1}{3}$

(B) $\frac{2}{3}$

(C) $\frac{3}{4}$

(D) 1

(E) 1 and $\frac{1}{4}$

30. How many cups of sugar should be used to make twelve servings?

(A) $\frac{1}{4}$

(B) $\frac{1}{3}$

(C) $\frac{2}{3}$

(D) $\frac{1}{2}$

(E) $\frac{3}{4}$

Average Cost of Hotel Rooms (Dollars)

MONTH

		Jan	Feb	Mar	Apr	May	Jun
	AK	192	114	102	125	179	150
	AL	91	96	122	101	125	146
STATE	CA	106	158	175	107	111	134
	DC	182	334	205	242	172	235
	MI	115	108	89	147	274	162
	VA	168	97	222	152	118	220

	Month	State	(A)	(B)	(C)	(D)	(E)
31.	Mar	CA	102	111	122	175	205
32.	Jun	AL	146	150	91	192	134
33.	Jan	AK	91	192	106	168	150
34.	Feb	VA	168	108	222	114	97
35.	May	DC	205	242	172	118	274

Dog Breed Comparisons

BORDER COLLIE	GREAT DANE	LABRADOR RETRIEVER	CHOW CHOW	AIREDALE	GERMAN SHEPHERD
Herding Dog	Working Dog	Sporting	Non-sporting	Terrier	Working/ Herding
Medium Size	Large Size	Medium Size	Medium Size	Medium Size	Large Size
Medium Coat	Short Coat	Short Coat	Long Coat	Medium Coat	Medium Coat
Eager to Please	Responds Well	Eager to Please	Independent	Eager to Please	Eager to Please
Weekly Grooming	Occasional Grooming	Occasional Grooming	Weekly Grooming	Weekly Grooming	Occasional Grooming
12 – 14 years expectancy	10 years expectancy	12 years expectancy	11 – 12 years expectancy	13 years expectancy	12 – 13 years expectancy
Older children	Any children	Any children	Requires socialization	Any children with supervision	Requires socialization

36. Which dog breed is considered part of the working and herding group?

   (A) border collie
   (B) chow chow
   (C) German shepherd
   (D) Great Dane
   (E) Labrador retriever

37. Which dog breed is considered a terrier?

   (A) Airedale
   (B) border collie
   (C) German shepherd
   (D) Great Dane
   (E) Labrador retriever

38. Which breed is medium size and has a long coat?

   (A) Airedale
   (B) chow chow
   (C) German shepherd
   (D) Great Dane
   (E) Labrador retriever

39. Which breed has only a ten-year life expectancy?

   (A) Airedale
   (B) border collie
   (C) German shepherd
   (D) Great Dane
   (E) Labrador retriever

40. Which dog breed is considered part of the sporting group?

   (A) Airedale
   (B) border collie
   (C) chow chow
   (D) Great Dane
   (E) Labrador retriever

INSTRUMENT COMPREHENSION

This part of the test measures your ability to determine the position of an airplane in flight from reading instruments showing its compass direction heading, amount of climb or dive, and degree of bank to right or left.

Each problem consists of two dials and four airplanes in flight. Your task is to determine which one of the four airplanes is most nearly in the position indicated by the two dials. You are always looking north at the same altitude as the four airplanes. East is always to your right as you look at the page.

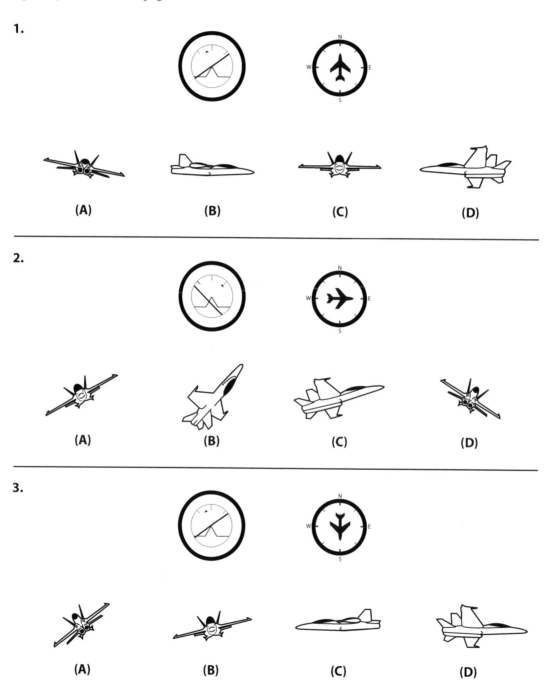

1.

(A)   (B)   (C)   (D)

2.

(A)   (B)   (C)   (D)

3.

(A)   (B)   (C)   (D)

4.

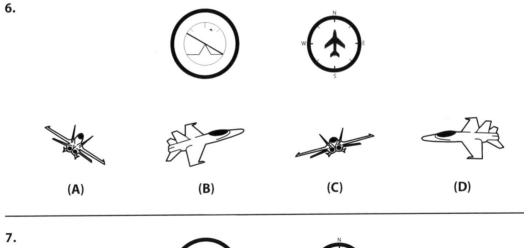

(A) (B) (C) (D)

5.

(A) (B) (C) (D)

6.

(A) (B) (C) (D)

7.

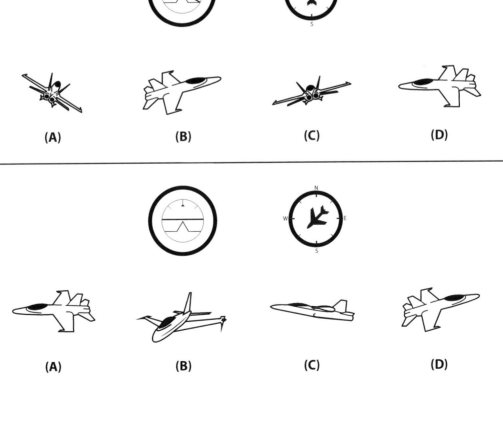

(A) (B) (C) (D)

8.

(A)   (B)   (C)   (D)

9.

(A)   (B)   (C)   (D)

10.

(A)   (B)   (C)   (D)

11.

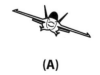

(A)   (B)   (C)   (D)

12.

(A)
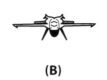
(B)
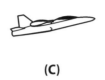
(C)

(D)

13.

(A)

(B)

(C)

(D)

14.

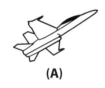
(A)

(B)

(C)

(D)

15.

(A)

(B)
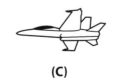
(C)

(D)

16.

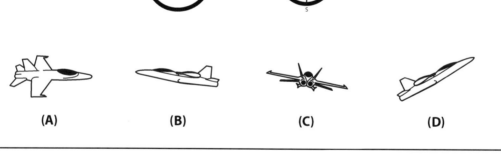

(A)   (B)   (C)   (D)

17.

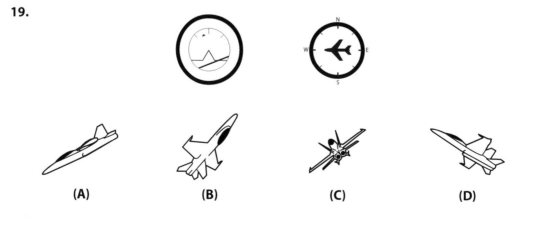

(A)   (B)   (C)   (D)

18.

(A)   (B)   (C)   (D)

19.

(A)   (B)   (C)   (D)

20.

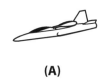 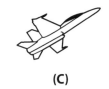

(A)   (B)   (C)   (D)

21.

   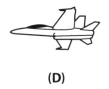

(A)   (B)   (C)   (D)

22.

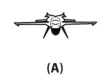 

(A)   (B)   (C)   (D)

23.

(A)   (B)   (C)   (D)

24.

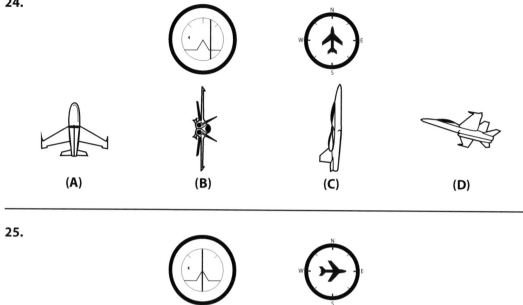

(A)   (B)   (C)   (D)

25.

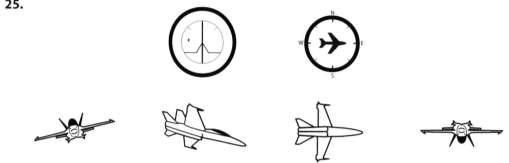

(A)   (B)   (C)   (D)

BLOCK COUNTING

Given a certain numbered block, your task is to determine how many other blocks the numbered block touches. Blocks are considered touching only if all or part of their faces touch. Blocks that only touch corners do not count. All of the blocks in each pile are the same size and shape.

Shape One

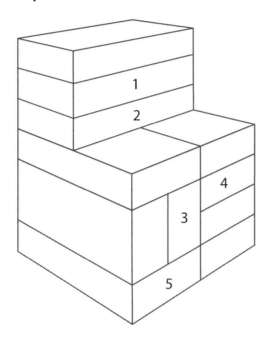

Shape Two

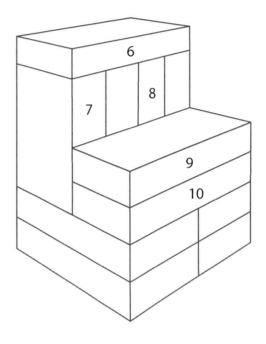

Block	A	B	C	D	E
1	1	3	2	5	4
2	3	2	1	4	5
3	5	3	4	2	6
4	2	3	5	6	4
5	8	7	4	3	2

Block	A	B	C	D	E
6	2	5	3	7	4
7	1	3	6	5	4
8	5	6	4	8	7
9	4	6	1	2	5
10	5	7	8	9	6

Shape Three

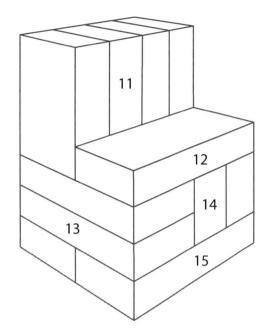

Shape Four

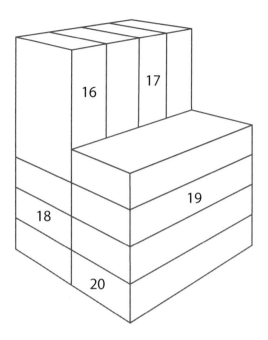

Block	A	B	C	D	E
11	3	4	5	6	2
12	8	4	3	5	7
13	5	3	4	6	7
14	6	7	8	3	4
15	4	3	6	7	5

Block	A	B	C	D	E
16	2	4	5	3	1
17	4	6	2	5	3
18	3	6	7	2	5
19	2	6	3	5	7
20	1	2	3	4	5

Shape Five

Shape Six

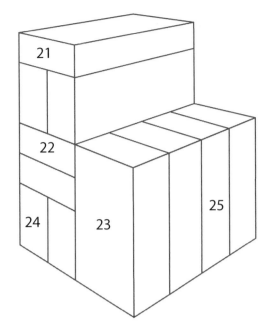

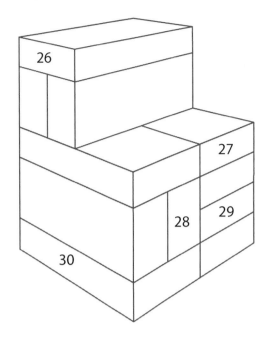

Block	A	B	C	D	E
21	3	2	5	6	2
22	8	4	3	5	7
23	4	3	5	6	7
24	6	2	8	3	4
25	4	2	5	7	6

Block	A	B	C	D	E
26	4	5	1	2	6
27	5	6	2	4	3
28	4	6	5	2	3
29	2	4	3	8	7
30	5	3	2	7	8

AVIATION INFORMATION

This part of the test measures your knowledge of aviation. Each of the questions or incomplete statements is followed by five choices. You are to decide which one of the choices best answers the question or completes the statement.

1. When the cyclic in a helicopter is pushed forward, what effect does that have on the rudder?

   (A) The rudder extends outward.

   (B) It has no effect.

   (C) The rudder shifts to the left.

   (D) The rudder shifts to the right.

   (E) The rudder tilts upward.

2. Which aircraft component(s) affect roll?

   (A) the ailerons

   (B) the ailerons and the spoilers

   (C) the elevators

   (D) the rudder

   (E) the rudder and the elevators

3. Which type of climb is made with the maximum power available?

   (A) a best angle of climb

   (B) a best rate of climb

   (C) a medium climb

   (D) a normal climb

   (E) a steep climb

4. What type of helicopter design uses a ducted fan in place of a tail rotor to cancel torque effect?

   (A) the coaxial rotor system

   (B) the NOTAR

   (C) the tandem rotor system

   (D) the semi-monocoque

   (E) the skids

5. When an aircraft is approaching to land, the leading and trailing edges of its flaps are extended to create the following force(s).

   (A) a decrease in drag

   (B) a decrease in lift

   (C) an increase in airspeed

   (D) an increase in airspeed and drag

   (E) maximum lift and high drag

6. When flying a helicopter, what response should be taken if the rpm is low and the manifold pressure is high?

   (A) increase the throttle

   (B) lower the collective pitch

   (C) move the cyclic forward

   (D) raise the collective pitch

   (E) reduce the throttle

7. Which aerodynamic force(s) must a rotary-wing aircraft balance in order to hover?

   (A) weight, lift, thrust, and drag

   (B) translational lift

   (C) dissymmetry of lift

   (D) gyroscopic precession

   (E) autorotation

8. If the ball on the turn and slip indicator is to the left or right, which flight control will return it to the center?

   (A) the cyclic or control wheel

   (B) the foot pedals

   (C) the pitot tube

   (D) resetting the altimeter

   (E) the throttle

9. Empennage refers to the
   (A) fuselage
   (B) landing gear section
   (C) propellers or rotor blades
   (D) tail section
   (E) wings

10. What part of the aircraft structure supports the tail rotor?
    (A) the teeter hinge
    (B) the swashplate
    (C) the ducted fan
    (D) the tail boom
    (E) the skids

11. Which is NOT considered part of the secondary flight control system?
    (A) the flaps
    (B) the leading edge devices
    (C) the rudder
    (D) the spoilers
    (E) the trim tabs

12. If magnetic north is a positive 15-degree variation (west) from true north, to convert true north to magnetic north when flying eastbound, what is the adjustment a pilot must make to the magnetic compass?
    (A) add 7.5 degrees
    (B) add 15 degrees
    (C) add 345 degrees
    (D) subtract 15 degrees
    (E) subtract 345 degrees

13. What direction will induced flow move during an autorotation?
    (A) horizontally
    (B) backward
    (C) parallel to the plane of rotation
    (D) to the right
    (E) vertically

14. What item was developed to reduce compass reading errors?
    (A) a heading indicator
    (B) low latitude charts
    (C) a three-pointer compass
    (D) sectional charts
    (E) a vertical card compass

15. Which is true in right-of-way protocol?
    (A) Any aircraft in distress always has the right-of-way.
    (B) Hot-air balloons always have the right-of-way over other aircraft.
    (C) Jets always have the right-of-way.
    (D) Powered parachutes always have the right-of-way.
    (E) The right-of-way protocol applies only in controlled airspaces.

16. Which instrument indicates if an aircraft is in a climb, in a descent, or in level flight?
    (A) an altimeter
    (B) a heading indicator
    (C) a magnetic compass
    (D) a vertical card compass
    (E) a vertical speed indicator

17. What defines unusable fuel?
    (A) fuel contaminated with oils
    (B) fuel in the tanks at delivery of an aircraft by the manufacturer
    (C) fuel not used (leftover) from any flight
    (D) fuel that cannot get to the engine
    (E) fuel spills

18. If the cyclic is moved forward, in which direction will the helicopter move?

(A) forward

(B) backward

(C) in circles

(D) left

(E) the nose will pitch up

19. What gives the pilot control over the yaw axis of the aircraft?

(A) the cyclic

(B) the collective

(C) the tail rotor pedals

(D) translating tendency

(E) the throttle

20. The altitude measured AGL is called _____.

(A) absolute altitude

(B) density altitude

(C) indicated altitude

(D) pressure altitude

(E) true altitude

ANSWER KEY

VERBAL ANALOGIES

1. **(C)**
   LABYRINTH is a synonym for MAZE; HIERARCHY is a synonym for LADDER.

2. **(E)**
   A TRIUMVIRATE is a group of 3 people; a QUARTET is a group of 4 people.

3. **(E)**
   The STOMACH'S main function is DIGESTION; the LUNGS' main function is RESPIRATION.

4. **(E)**
   INEPTITUDE and AMPLITUDE share the ending -itude; WISTFULNESS and BLAMELESSNESS share the suffix -ness. Each of these endings can change an adjective (INEPT, AMPLE, WISTFUL, BLAMELESS) to a noun.

5. **(D)**
   Intense FEELING can be called FERVOR; an intensely held OPINION can be called a CONVICTION.

6. **(A)**
   BELITTLE is an antonym for PRAISE; GALVANIZE is an antonym for BORE.

7. **(C)**
   Extreme DISLIKE can be called RANCOR; extreme TIREDNESS can be called EXHAUSTION.

8. **(E)**
   A PEBBLE is a small rock, while a BOULDER is a huge one; a HUT is a small building, while a CASTLE is a huge one.

9. **(B)**
   An INCH is a shorter unit of measurement than a FOOT; a CENTIMETER is a shorter unit of measurement than a METER.

10. **(D)**
    A FEW items means a small number, while COUNTLESS items means a huge number; a BRIEF amount of time goes by quickly, while an INTERMINABLE amount of time seems to go on forever.

11. (C)

ABBERATION is a synonym for DEVIATION; ICONOCLAST is a synonym for REBEL.

12. (B)

A person uses a KNIFE for SLICING food; he or she uses a FORK for PIERCING food.

13. (D)

A SENTENCE is part of a PARAGRAPH; a STANZA is part of a POEM.

14. (D)

EXCRUCIATING and EXTRAORDINARY share the prefix ex–; DEBILITATE and DECONSTRUCT share the prefix de–.

15. (A)

BLITHE is a synonym for CHEERFUL; CALLOUS is a synonym for INSENSTIVE.

16. (B)

A SEAGULL is one member of a FLOCK; a WOLF is one member of a PACK.

17. (B)

CACHE is a synonym for HOARD; KINDLE is a synonym for IGNITE.

18. (C)

A SINGER is one member of a CHOIR; a MUSICIAN is one member of a BAND.

19. (A)

A KNUCKLE is part of a person's FINGER; an ELBOW is part of a person's ARM.

20. (E)

A TABLESPOON is a much smaller unit of liquid measurement than a GALLON; a METER is a much shorter unit of measurement for length or distance than a KILOMETER.

21. (B)

A QUARTER is 0.25 times one dollar; a DIME is 0.1 times one dollar.

22. (B)

A KEYBOARD is part of a COMPUTER; a BURNER is part of a STOVE.

23. (C)

HACKNEYED is an antonym for ORIGINAL; ECLECTIC is an antonym for UNVARIED.

24. (B)

A CRUMB of bread is one tiny piece of a LOAF; a DROP of water is one tiny part of a GALLON.

25. (A)

A MILE is a unit of measurement that measures DISTANCE; a POUND is a unit of measurement that measures WEIGHT.

1. (E)

Use the formula for percentages.

$part = whole \times percent = 540 \times 0.85 =$ **459**

2. (C)

total seats $= 4500 + 2000$

$\dfrac{\text{lower seats}}{\text{all seats}} = \dfrac{4,500}{6,500} = \dfrac{9}{13}$

3. (B)

Use the combination formula to find the number of ways to choose 2 people out of a group of 20.

$C(20, 2) = \dfrac{20!}{2!\,18!} = $ **190**

4. (A)

Multiply by the converstion factor to get from pounds to kilograms.

8 pounds, 8 ounces = 8.5 pounds

$8.5 \text{ lb.} \left(\dfrac{1 \text{ kg}}{2.2 \text{ lb.}} \right) = $ **3.9 kg**

5. (D)

Find the amount of change and add to the original amount.

$amount\ of\ change = original\ amount \times percent\ change$

$= 37,500 \times 0.055 = 2,062.50$

$37,500 + 2,062.50 = $ **\$39,562.50**

6. (C)

Add the value of the three cars.

$15,000 + 2(12,900) = 40,800$

Use the formula for percentages to find the total commission.

$part = whole \times percent$

$= 40,800 \times 0.02 = $ **\$816**

7. (C)

If each student receives 2 notebooks, the teacher will need $16 \times 2 = 32$ notebooks. After handing out the notebooks, she will have $50 - 32 = $ **18 notebooks left**.

8. (C)

Use the equation for percentages.

$whole = \dfrac{part}{percentage} = \dfrac{17}{0.4} = $ **42.5**

9. (A)

Convert each value into minutes, and use the formula for percentages to find the time spent running sprints.

$percent = \dfrac{part}{whole}$

$= \dfrac{15}{60 + 30 + 15} = 0.143 = $ **14.3%**

10. (A)

Add the number of cupcakes he will give to his friend and to his coworkers, then subtract that value from 48.

\# of cupcakes for his friend:

$\dfrac{1}{2} \times 48 = 24$

\# of cupcakes for his coworkers:

$\dfrac{1}{3} \times 48 = 16$

$48 - (24 + 16) = $ **8**

11. (C)

Use the law of sines.

$\dfrac{\sin 20°}{14} = \dfrac{\sin 100°}{x}$

$x = \dfrac{14(\sin 100°)}{\sin 20°}$

$x = $ **40.31**

12. (B)

There are 15 minutes between 7:45 a.m. and 8:00 a.m. and 20 minutes between 8:00 a.m. and 8:20 a.m.

15 minutes + 20 minutes = **35 minutes**

13. (B)

Set up a proportion. Cube the scale factor when calculating volume.

$\dfrac{54\pi}{x} = \dfrac{3^3}{4^3}$

$x = $ **128π**

14. (D)

One way to find the answer is to draw a picture.

Put 24 cans into groups of 4. One out of every 4 cans is diet (light gray) so there is 1 light gray can for every 3 dark gray cans. That leaves 18 dark gray cans (regular soda).

Alternatively, solve the problem using ratios.

$\frac{Regular}{Total} = \frac{3}{4} = \frac{x}{24}$

$4x = 72$

$x = 18$

15. (C)

Set up a proportion and solve. Add the parts of the ratio together to find the whole.

$\frac{1}{3+2+1} = \frac{3}{6} = \frac{x}{500,000}$

$3(500,000) = 6x$

$x = \$250,000$

16. (A)

p = number of pages written by Chris

$2p$ = number of pages written by Kim

$p + 2p = 240$

$p = 80$

17. (D)

$\frac{150\ cm}{1} \times \frac{10\ mm}{1\ cm} = 1500\ mm$

18. (B)

Set up an equation to find the number of orders of chicken strips they can afford:

$\$10 - 2(\$2.00 + \$1.00) = x$

$\$10 - 2(\$3.00) = x$

$\$10 - \$6.00 = \$4.00$

Four dollars is enough money to buy 1 order of chicken strips to share.

19. (D)

Find the amount the store owner paid for the refrigerators.

$850 \times 30 = 25,500$

Find the amount the owner will earn for the refrigerators.

sale price = $850(1.15) = 977.50$

$977.50 \times 30 = 29,325$

Subtract the amount the owner paid from the amount he earned to find his profits.

$29,325 - 25,500 = \$3,825$

20. (C)

Use the formula for finding percentages. Express the percentage as a decimal.

$part = whole \times percentage = \mathbf{1560 \times 0.15}$

21. (D)

Use the formula for an arithmetic sum.

$S_n = \frac{n}{2}(2a_1 + (n-1)d)$

$= \frac{25}{2}(2(14) + (25-1)2) = 950$

22. (B)

Find the sum of the 13 numbers whose mean is 30.

$13 \times 30 = 390$

Find the sum of the 8 numbers whose mean is 42.

$8 \times 42 = 336$

Find the sum and mean of the remaining 5 numbers.

$390 - 336 = 54$

$\frac{54}{5} = 10.8$

23. (D)

Use the formula for percentages.

$percent = \frac{part}{whole}$

$= \frac{42}{48}$

$= 0.875 = 87.5\%$

24. (C)

Use the equation for probability.

$probability = \frac{possible\ favorable\ outcomes}{all\ possible\ outcomes}$

$= \frac{7}{(5+7+8)}$

$= \frac{7}{20}$

25. (D)

Set up a proportion and solve.

$\frac{1\ in.}{25\ miles} = \frac{x\ in.}{115\ miles}$

$1(115) = 25x$

$x = 4.6\ inches$

WORD KNOWLEDGE

1. **(C)**

   Substantial means "an ample or considerable amount." For example, wealthy people have a substantial amount of money.

2. **(A)**

   The word root *ācer* in *acrid, acrimony,* and *acrimonious* means "sharp and sour," and the suffix *–ous* means "possessing or full of." And so, an acrimonious relationship is full of bitterness.

3. **(C)**

   Inclement weather is stormy, windy, blustery, or otherwise severe.

4. **(D)**

   The word root *concili* means "council," the suffix *–ate* means "perform the action of," and the suffix *–ory* means "characterized by." And so, a conciliatory person is one who councils others to make peace.

5. **(A)**

   Taciturn means "reluctant or unwilling to talk." For example, a taciturn person may appear shy or uninterested in socializing with others.

6. **(E)**

   The prefix *con–* means "with or together," the word root *concurrere* means "to run together," and the suffix *–ent* means "doing a certain action." And so, two or more concurrent events happen at the same time, or simultaneously.

7. **(A)**

   Elusive means "hard to understand or identify." For example, in a mystery story, the solution to the crime may be elusive, or difficult to discover.

8. **(C)**

   The prefix *com–* means "in association with," the word root *plex* means "to fold together," and the suffix *–ity* means "the act or condition of." And so, complicity is the act of working with someone on something—and sometimes that something is a crime.

9. **(B)**

   Relegate means "dismiss or downgrade."

10. **(C)**

    The prefix *mono–* means "one," the word root *lith* means "stone," and the suffix *–ic* means "having some of the characteristics of." A monolith is a huge statue made from one stone, so a monolithic object is huge or colossal, like a monolith is.

11. **(C)**

    Lampoon means "to ridicule through satire." For example, political cartoons lampoon public figures by exaggerating and poking fun at their flaws and misdeeds.

12. **(D)**

    The word root *pater* means "father," and the word root *arkhein* means "to rule," so a patriarch is a man who leads his family.

13. **(E)**

    Sensory means "relating to the senses, including sight, sound, taste, smell, and touch." For example, someone experiencing sensory overload is receiving too much information through his senses.

14. **(E)**

    The word root *quāl* means "of what sort," and the suffix *–ive* means "indicating a certain character," so a qualitative report evaluates someone or something based on qualities or characteristics.

15. (C)

Obsequious means "to show flattering attention." For example, an obsequious employee always defers to his boss and will do anything he is asked.

16. (B)

Noxious means "physically or morally harmful." For example, a noxious gas can be lethal to people and animals.

17. (D)

The prefix *mis–* means "negating," the word root *anthropos* means "man or people," and the suffix *–ic* means "having certain traits." And so, a *misanthrope* or misanthropic person is someone who distrusts and dislikes most other people.

18. (E)

The word root *fēlīx* means "happy," and the suffix *–ity* means "the act or condition of," so felicity is contentment, joy, or happiness.

19. (B)

The word root *chevalier* means "noble, brave, faithful knight," and the suffix *–ous* means "possessing the traits of," so a chivalrous person is brave, considerate, kind, and polite, especially to those who need protection.

20. (A)

The prefix *ex–* means "out of or from," the word root *proprius* means "someone's possession," and the suffix *–ate* means "perform the action of." And so, to expropriate an item means to take it from the person it belongs to or to steal it.

21. (D)

Ebb means "to fall or recede." For example, when an ocean tide ebbs, it recedes from shore.

22. (B)

The word root *icon* means "image," and the word root *klast* means "to break." An image breaker is someone who rebels against established religion or leadership.

23. (C)

Pragmatic means "related to practical matters." For example, a pragmatic person evaluates the facts and makes a realistic plan before acting.

24. (A)

The word root *kak* means "evil," and the word root *phone* means "sound," so cacophony is the opposite of harmony; it is a combination of harsh, unpleasant noises that sound terrible together.

25. (A)

To cajole means to wheedle, coax, or entice someone into doing something. For example, a child might cajole her parents into buying her ice cream.

MATH KNOWLEDGE

1. **(D)**

Use the formula for the volume of a sphere to find its radius.

$V = \frac{4}{3}\pi r^3$

$972\pi = \frac{4}{3}\pi r^3$

$r = 9$

Use the super Pythagorean theorem to find the side of the cube.

$d^2 = a^2 + b^2 + c^2$

$18^2 = 3s^2$

$s \approx 10.4$

Use the length of the side to find the volume of the cube.

$V = s^3$

$V \approx (10.4)^3$

$V \approx \mathbf{1125}$

2. **(C)**

Convert each fraction to the LCD and subtract the numerators.

$\frac{7}{8} - \frac{1}{10} - \frac{2}{3}$

$= \frac{7}{8}\left(\frac{15}{15}\right) - \frac{1}{10}\left(\frac{12}{12}\right) - \frac{2}{3}\left(\frac{40}{40}\right)$

$= \frac{105}{120} - \frac{12}{120} - \frac{80}{120} = \mathbf{\frac{13}{120}}$

3. **(B)**

Plug 4 in for j and simplify.

$2(j - 4)^4 - j + \frac{1}{2}j$

$2(4 - 4)^4 - 4 + \frac{1}{2}(4) = \mathbf{-2}$

4. **(B)**

Isolate the variable y on one side of the equation.

$3y + 2x = 15z$

$3y = -2x + 15z$

$\mathbf{y = \frac{-2x + 15z}{3}}$

5. **(C)**

Factor the expression using the greatest common factor of 3.

$54z^4 + 18z^3 + 3z + 3 =$

$\mathbf{3(18z^4 + 6z^3 + z + 1)}$

6. **(D)**

Find the area of the square as if it did not have the corners cut out.

$12 \text{ mm} \times 12 \text{ mm} = 144 \text{ mm}^2$

Find the area of the four cut out corners.

$2 \text{ mm} \times 2 \text{ mm} = 4 \text{ mm}^2$

$4(4 \text{ mm}^2) = 16 \text{ mm}^2$

Subtract the area of the cut out corners from the large square to find the area of the shape.

$144 \text{ mm}^2 - 16 \text{ mm}^2 = \mathbf{128 \text{ mm}^2}$

7. **(D)**

Set up a system of equations and solve using elimination.

f = the cost of a financial stock

a = the cost of an auto stock

$50f + 10a = 1300$

$10f + 10a = 500$

$\qquad 50f + 10a = 1300$

$\underline{+ \; -50f - 50a = -2500}$

$\qquad\qquad -40a = -1,200$

$\qquad\qquad\qquad a = 30$

$50(30) = \mathbf{1,500}$

8. **(A)**

Isolate the variable x on one side.

$4x + 12 = x - 3$

$3x = -15$

$\mathbf{x = -5}$

9. **(C)**

Use the rules of exponents to simplify the expression.

$\left(\frac{4x^{-3}y^4z}{8x^{-5}y^3z^{-2}}\right)^2 = \left(\frac{x^2yz^3}{2}\right)^2 = \mathbf{\frac{x^4y^2z^6}{4}}$

10. **(C)**

The greatest distance will be between two points at opposite ends of each sphere's diameters. Find the diameter of each sphere and add them.

$36\pi = \frac{4}{3}\pi r_1^3$

$r_1 = 3$

$d_1 = 2(3) = 6$

$288\pi = \frac{4}{3}\pi r_2^3$

$r_2 = 6$

$d_2 = 2(6) = 12$

$d_1 + d_1 = 6 + 12 = \mathbf{18}$

11. (C)

Factor the greatest common factor $2ab$ out of both terms.

$4a3b + 10ab^2 = \mathbf{2ab(2a^2 + 5b)}$

12. (A)

The 8 is in the thousands place. Because the value to the right of the 8 is less than 5, the 8 remains the same and all values to its right become zero. The result is **498,000**.

13. (C)

Plug 0 in for x and solve for y.

$7y - 42x + 7 = 0$

$7y - 42(0) + 7 = 0$

$y = -1$

The y-intercept is at **(0, −1)**.

14. (A)

Use FOIL to distribute.

$(3 + \sqrt{2})(3 - \sqrt{2}) =$

$3(3) + 3(-\sqrt{2}) + \sqrt{2}(3) + \sqrt{2}(-\sqrt{2})$

$= 9 - 3\sqrt{2} + 3\sqrt{2} - 2 = \mathbf{7}$

15. (D)

Set up a proportion to find the weight of the removed wedge.

$\frac{60°}{x \text{ lb.}} = \frac{360°}{73 \text{ lb.}}$

$x \approx 12.17$ lb.

Subtract the removed wedge from the whole to find the weight of the remaining piece.

$73 - 12.17 = \mathbf{60.83}$

16. (D)

Plug in each set of values and determine if the inequality is true.

$2(0) + 0 \leq -10$ FALSE

$2(10) + 2 \leq -10$ FALSE

$2(10) + 10 \leq -10$ FALSE

$2(-10) + (-10) \leq -10$ TRUE

$2(0) + 10 \leq -10$ FALSE

17. (C)

$6(3^0) = 6(1) = \mathbf{6}$

18. (D)

The sum of the internal angles of a quadrilateral is **360°**.

19. (E)

Use FOIL to solve.

$(3x + 2)(3x + 2) = 9x^2 + 6x + 6x + 4 = \mathbf{9x^2 + 12x + 4}$

20. (D)

Use the volume to find the length of the cube's side.

$V = s^3$

$343 = s^3$

$s = 7$ m

Find the area of each side and multiply by 6 to find the total surface area.

$7(7) = 49$ m

$49(6) = \mathbf{294 \text{ m}^2}$

21. (D)

Use the distance formula.

$d = \sqrt{(x_2 - x_1)^2 + (y_2 - y_1)^2}$

$= \sqrt{(-2 - 3)^2 + (-5 - 0)^2} = \sqrt{50} = \mathbf{5\sqrt{2}}$

22. (A)

Substitute 8 for x and 2 for y in the expression.

$3x + 7y - 4$

$3(8) + 7(2) - 4 = 24 + 14 - 4 = \mathbf{34}$

23. (B)

Use the Pythagorean theorem to determine which set of values forms a right triangle.

$40^2 + 41^2 = 50^2$

$3,281 \neq 2,500$

$9^2 + 40^2 = 41^2$

$\mathbf{1,681 = 1,681}$

$9^2 + 30^2 = 40^2$

$981 \neq 1,600$

$40^2 + 50^2 = 63^2$

$4{,}100 \neq 3{,}969$

$40^2 + 41^2 = 63^2$

$3{,}281 \neq 3{,}969$

24. (C)

Plug the given values into the equation and solve for t.

$d = v \times t$

$4000 = 500 \times t$

$t = 8$ hours

25. (E)

Multiply the constants and add the exponents on each variable.

$3(6) = 18$

$x^2(x) = x^3$

$y(y^3) = y^4$

$z^4(z^2) = z^6$

$3x^2yz^4(6xy^3z^2) = \mathbf{18x^3y^4z^6}$

READING COMPREHENSION

1.   (D)

(A) is incorrect. While this is a conclusion drawn in the passage, it is not the main idea.

(B) is incorrect. This is not the main idea of the passage.

(C) is incorrect. While this is stated in the passage, it is not the main idea.

(D) is correct. The author writes, "it was not until the Vietnam War that the military began to rely on helicopters both as transport tools and offensive weapons."

(E) is incorrect. This point is made only at the end of the passage.

2.   (E)

(A) is incorrect. The passage states, "The Viet Cong modeled their military strategy after Mao Zedong's successful guerilla movement in China."

(B) is incorrect. The passage states, "Because they did not need long landing strips, helicopters were able to navigate the treacherous mountains and extract the flight crews."

(C) is incorrect. The passage states, "The United States faced a new military challenge: How to defeat an enemy that avoided confrontation?"

(D) is incorrect. The passage states that "crew members began to carry rifles to shoot at combatants in defense."

(E) is correct. The passage states, "This success bolstered American military interest in helicopters and led to investment in building US supply. As a result, during the Korean War, use of helicopters expanded."

3.   (C)

(A) is incorrect. The passage explains that while the United States believed itself to have military superiority, it was unprepared for the Viet Cong's tactics.

(B) is incorrect. Although the passage does not discuss air assaults until the final paragraph in relation to Afghanistan, the author states that similar guerilla techniques were first used in Vietnam.

(C) is correct. The passage states that "during the Korean War, use of helicopters expanded from extraction of downed crews to medical evacuations."

(D) is incorrect. In the first sentence, the author mentions Agent Orange and napalm in describing other military tools used in Vietnam.

(E) is incorrect. The author states that the US military focused heavily on building bases, but the Viet Cong did not.

4.   (B)

(A) is incorrect. The author argues that the US was ill-prepared for the war in Vietnam.

(B) is correct. The author explains that the Viet Cong fought unlike enemies American troops had previously faced.

(C) is incorrect. The passage discusses the importance of helicopters to the wars in Afghanistan and Iraq, neither of which have jungle terrain.

(D) is incorrect. While the author states that helicopters are highly valued, they do not compare them to other tools used in combat.

(E) is incorrect. The passage does not discuss the Viet Cong's use of helicopters.

5. **(A)**

    (A) is correct. The passage states that the "Viet Cong infiltrated the jungles and its villages by blending in with the local population and winning their allegiance."

    (B) is incorrect. There is no context that implies the Viet Cong were suffering.

    (C) is incorrect. There is no context that implies a large number of people were relocating from one place to another.

    (D) is incorrect. The passage states that the Viet Cong "infiltrated" the jungle, not that they avoided it.

    (E) is incorrect. The passage states that the Viet Cong gained the villages' allegiance, making it clear that they did not attempt to control the villages; they already had their loyalty.

6. **(A)**

    (A) is correct. The passage states, "The versatility of helicopters has made them one of the most valued assets in the modern military."

    (B) is incorrect. The author describes the United States' increased reliance on helicopters but does not argue that it is a problem.

    (C) is incorrect. Nothing in the passage addresses the helicopters' impact on the number of soldiers killed.

    (D) is incorrect. The author does not discuss current military investment in helicopters, and the author believes helicopters are an important tool.

    (E) is incorrect. The author argues that the arming of helicopters was one of the most significant developments to come out of the Vietnam War.

7. **(D)**

    (A) is incorrect. The passage does this as part of the primary theme about the consequences of nuclear war; the damage to the ozone is just one of the consequences discussed.

    (B) is incorrect. No comparisons are made in the passage. Both topics relate to threats to the health of people for generations as a result of a nuclear war.

    (C) is incorrect. The passage gives details about this, but it is not the primary concern.

    (D) is correct. The passage provides the results of a study about the effects of a large-scale nuclear detonation on the ozone layer and a summary of the effects of the Castle/Bravo detonation.

    (E) is incorrect. The passage begins by reporting that it has been more than a decade since testing of nuclear weapons was done by the great powers.

8. **(A)**

    (A) is correct. The Arms Control and Disarmament Agency is working toward that goal.

    (B) is incorrect. The passage does not mention this. It seems unlikely to happen as long as other countries have nuclear weapons; however, many officials are working towards nuclear disarmament.

    (C) is incorrect. The passage indicates that the great powers have stopped this.

    (D) is incorrect. This statement is inaccurate; the focus of the passage is nuclear war, not nuclear power. Although the evidence indicates that the production should be halted, it is the detonation, not the production that creates the aftereffects.

    (E) is incorrect. While the author might agree with this statement, the passage focuses primarily on the consequences of the use of nuclear weapons, not consequences of their production.

9. **(B)**

(A) is incorrect. The author does not indicate that this phrasing is dehumanizing. The part that is dehumanizing is the method of referring to a full nuclear war as an "exchange."

(B) is correct. Instead of saying nuclear war, the strategists use the term "exchange." This is dehumanizing because it minimizes the horrific suffering and devastation to human life that would be caused by large-scale detonations.

(C) is incorrect. The "exchange" apparently would be a war with both sides using nuclear weapons. A war is greater than a large-scale detonation, which may involve use of a nuclear weapon by only one group.

(D) is incorrect. This agency is working to stop or prevent the production and use of nuclear weapons.

(E) is incorrect. Studies have indicated that large-scale detonations would eliminate portions of the ozone layer, which would result in increased ultraviolet radiation that leads to such conditions as "incapacitating" sunburns and snow blindness. These are facts, however. What is dehumanizing is the lack of recognition of the "fearsome consequence" of large-scale use of nuclear weapons.

10. **(B)**

(A) is incorrect. The author is presenting scientific research objectively, but is not indifferent. The author's concern is apparent in the statement, "large-scale nuclear war could produce casualties on a colossal scale, far beyond the local effects of blast and fire alone."

(B) is correct. The author presents fact after fact of the dire consequences and serious threat of nuclear detonations, creating the cumulative effect of an urgent warning.

(C) is incorrect. The force of facts suggests that the author has no confusion about what people need to know.

(D) is incorrect. The author seems to be suggesting that there is time and hope that the Arms Control and Disarmament Agency will prevent the looming despair of nuclear war.

(E) is incorrect. The author is completely committed to the goals of the Arms Control and Disarmament Agency.

11. **(E)**

(A) is incorrect. The problem of nuclear war is made clear in terms of the consequences; however, no solution is mentioned.

(B) is incorrect. The term is mentioned in the introduction as a lead in to the idea that there is extensive knowledge of the technology, but knowledge of the consequences is evolving.

(C) is incorrect. The passage focuses not on the nuclear war itself but on the consequences of nuclear war.

(D) is incorrect. The second part of the passage mentions one detonation of the twentieth century, and the first part explains the results of studies conducted on the consequences of nuclear war.

(E) is correct. First, the results of the study conducted by the National Academy of Science are explained; then, the discoveries from a study of the results of the 1954 nuclear detonation are detailed.

12. **(A)**

(A) is correct. The passage states, "More than any other event in the decade of testing large nuclear weapons in the atmosphere, Castle/Bravo's unexpected contamination of 7,000 square miles of the Pacific Ocean dramatically illustrated how large-scale nuclear war could produce casualties on a colossal scale."

(B) is incorrect. Although some people may think this, there is no mention of such a view, only facts about the devastating consequences.

(C) is incorrect. There is no ban, although many are hoping for one that can be enforced.

(D) is incorrect. The passage does not include information on nuclear material.

(E) is incorrect. There is no mention of this controversy; however, the author treats this detonation as extremely significant.

13. **(C)**

(A) is incorrect. This option allows for the possibility of recovery, which suggests a return to the way things were before the war. Global changes are more permanent and serious.

(B) is incorrect. The assumption is that the war would probably take place in this hemisphere, but the passage states that 30–70 percent of the ozone layer would be eliminated in the north, not the hemisphere itself.

(C) is correct. Global changes are the result of large-scale detonations, according to the study by the Academy of Sciences.

(D) is incorrect. The passage does point out that imbalances would occur, but it does not mention panic.

(E) is incorrect. The passage indicates the probability that the nuclear war would be fought in the north, so the effects would be lessened in the south.

14. **(A)**

(A) is correct. Truman says, "To ensure the peaceful development of nations, free from coercion, the United States has taken a leading part in establishing the United Nations [...] We shall not realize our objectives, however, unless we are willing to help free peoples to maintain their free institutions and their national integrity against aggressive movements that seek to impose upon them totalitarian regimes."

(B) is incorrect. Truman does not describe the brutality of the regimes that threaten the independence of other nations; he only specifies that the regimes are imposed against the will of the people.

(C) is incorrect. Truman does not describe the cruelty of the regimes that threaten the independence of other nations; he only specifies that the regimes are imposed against the will of the people.

(D) is incorrect. This answer choice does not fit in the context of the sentence.

(E) is incorrect. Truman does not indicate that the countries of the world are angry.

15. **(C)**

(A) is incorrect. Truman does not indicate that he is reminding America of its existing stance on foreign intervention.

(B) is incorrect. Truman does not seek to reassure Americans of the country's strength.

(C) is correct. Truman states, "This was a fundamental issue in the war with Germany and Japan. Our victory was won over countries which sought to impose their will, and their way of life, upon other nations." Later, he says, "At the present moment in world history nearly every nation must choose between alternative ways of life. The choice is too often not a free one."

(D) is incorrect. Truman seeks to draw a comparison—not a contrast—between the present situation and the one that led to America's intervention in the war.

(E) is incorrect. Truman does not seek to create apprehension about America's future, only to suggest that the country should intervene on behalf of other countries whose futures are less clear.

16. **(D)**

(A) is incorrect. Truman draws the contrast not to advocate for democracy but to highlight the gravity of the situations in those countries whose governments "[rely] on terror and oppression, a controlled press and radio; fixed elections, and the suppression of personal freedoms."

(B) is incorrect. Truman gives no indication that he is addressing the tyrannical leaders of oppressed nations or that he hopes to change their behaviors.

(C) is incorrect. Though Truman does mention the reasons America might consider intervening, he does not describe or go into detail about them.

(D) is correct. Truman states that "every nation must choose between alternative ways of life" and that "[t]he choice is too often not a free one." He then goes on to say that "it must be the policy of the United States to support free people who are resisting attempted subjugation by armed minorities or by outside pressures."

(E) is incorrect. Truman indicates that his concern is with "assisting free peoples to work out their own destinies[,]" not with the freedom of American itself.

17. **(A)**

(A) is correct. This choice addresses all of the main ideas of the passage: the flu is potentially deadly, highly infectious, and difficult to contain due to viral shedding.

(B) is incorrect. While this detail is included in the passage, it is not the main idea.

(C) is incorrect. While this detail is included in the passage, it is not the main idea.

(D) is incorrect. While this detail is included in the passage, it is not the main idea.

(E) is incorrect. While this detail is included in the passage, it is not the main idea.

18. **(D)**

(A) is incorrect. According to the passage, "the flu is not actually highly infectious" and "many people who contract the virus will recover[.]"

(B) is incorrect. According to the passage, "many people who contract the virus will recover[.]"

(C) is incorrect. According to the passage, "the flu is not actually highly infectious, meaning it's relatively difficult to contract."

(D) is correct. According to the passage, "the flu is...relatively difficult to contract[,]" and "[w]hile many people who contract the virus will recover, many others will not."

(E) is incorrect. According to the passage, "the flu is...relatively difficult to contract[,]" and "many [people who contract the virus] will not [recover]."

19. **(C)**

(A) is incorrect. The term *infectious* refers to the relative ease or difficulty of transmission; the number of people who end up dying as a result is not relevant to the question.

(B) is incorrect. This choice explains why the flu is difficult to contain but does not explain why the flu is not considered highly infectious.

(C) is correct. The second paragraph states that the flu is "relatively difficult to contract" because it "can only be transmitted when individuals come into direct contact with bodily fluids of people infected with the flu or when they are exposed to expelled aerosol particles[.]"

(D) is incorrect. The author mentions viral shedding and symptom development rates to illustrate why the flu is difficult to contain, but this does not explain why it is considered to not be highly infectious.

(E) is incorrect. Symptom development does not make a disease infectious or not infectious in terms of the actual transmission of the virus.

20. **(A)**

(A) is correct. The author uses the term *measures* to describe the steps that people to take to prevent the spreading of the influenza virus.

(B) is incorrect. This answer choice does not fit in the context of the sentence.

(C) is incorrect. This answer choice does not fit in the context of the sentence.

(D) is incorrect. This answer choice does not fit in the context of the sentence.

(E) is incorrect. This answer choice does not fit in the context of the sentence.

21. **(C)**

(A) is incorrect. The first paragraph of the passage states, "Over the past 150 years, tens of millions of people have died from the flu, and millions more have been left with lingering complications such as secondary infections."

(B) is incorrect. The final paragraph of the passage states, "Viral shedding—the process by which the body releases viruses that have been successfully reproducing during the infection—takes place two days after infection, while symptoms do not usually develop until the third day of infection. Thus, infected individuals have at least twenty-four hours in which they may unknowingly infect others."

(C) is correct. The final paragraph of the passage states that viral shedding is "the process by which the body releases viruses that have been successfully reproducing during the infection[.]"

(D) is incorrect. The second paragraph of the passage states that "[t]he flu can only be transmitted when individuals come into direct contact with bodily fluids of people infected with the flu or when they are exposed to expelled aerosol particles[.]"

(E) is incorrect. The second paragraph of the passage states that "the viruses can only travel short distances as aerosol particles and will die within a few hours on hard surfaces[.]"

22. **(A)**

(A) is correct. The second paragraph of the passage states that "the virus can be contained with fairly simple health measures like hand washing and face masks."

(B) is incorrect. The second paragraph contains information about how the influenza virus is spread and how people can prevent against it.

(C) is incorrect. Though the flu can be deadly, the passage states that "the flu is not actually highly infectious, meaning it's relatively difficult to contract."

(D) is incorrect. The passage indicates that viral shedding begins "two days after infection" but does not indicate for how long infected individuals can continue to infect others.

(E) is incorrect. The passage indicates that even though the flu is not very highly infectious, it "has historically been one of the most common, and deadliest, human infections" and that people should attempt to protect themselves from the virus using "fairly simple health measures like hand washing and face masks."

23. **(D)**

(A) is incorrect. In regional studies, geographers "examine the characteristics of a particular place[.]"

(B) is incorrect. In topical studies, geographers "look at a single physical or human feature that impacts the world[.]"

(C) is incorrect. In physical studies, geographers "focus on the physical features of Earth[.]"

(D) is correct. The passage describes human studies as the study of "the relationship between human activity and the environment," which would include farmers interacting with river systems.

(E) is incorrect. In physical studies, geographers "focus on the physical features of Earth," not human activity.

24. **(A)**

(A) is correct. The passage explains what the study of geography involves and outlines its main sub-disciplines.

(B) Incorrect. The passage does not include a story.

(C) is incorrect. The passage does not seek to change readers' opinions or behaviors.

(D) is incorrect. The passage provides information and facts but not descriptive details.

(E) is incorrect. The passage relies on factual information, not emotional or logical arguments.

25. **(B)**

(A) is incorrect. This is only one fact from the passage and does not represent an adequate summary of the passage as a whole.

(B) is correct. Only this choice summarizes the two main points of the passage: the definition of geography and the breakdown of its sub-disciplines.

(C) is incorrect. This is only one detail from the passage and does not represent an adequate summary of the passage as a whole.

(D) is incorrect. This choice summarizes the second paragraph only and leaves out any summary of the first paragraph.

(E) is incorrect. Though this statement is implied by the passage, it does not adequately summarize the passage as a whole.

PHYSICAL SCIENCE

1. (A)

(A) is correct. Energy is measured in joules.

(B) is incorrect. Power is measured in watts.

(C) is incorrect. Force is measured in newtons.

(D) is incorrect. Displacement (or distance) is measured in meters.

(E) is incorrect. Frequency is measured in hertz.

2. (E)

(A) is incorrect. *Aurora* is the phenomenon of colored lights that appears in the sky near the North and South Poles.

(B) is incorrect. The galaxy is a large group of stars held together by gravity.

(C) is incorrect. Black holes are collapsed stars whose gravitational pull is so strong that light cannot escape.

(D) is incorrect. Eclipses occur when the earth, moon, and sun align.

(E) is correct. Before a star collapses, the star burns brighter for a period of time and then fades from view. This is a supernova.

3. (B)

(A) is incorrect. The amplitude is the distance from the wave's midline to its crest or trough.

(B) is correct. Wavelength is the length of each cycle of the wave, which can be found by measuring between crests.

(C) is incorrect. Frequency is the number of cycles a wave passes through during a time period.

(D) is incorrect. Period is the time it takes for a wave to complete one cycle.

(E) is incorrect. *Pitch* is another term for *frequency* and describes how high or low a wave sounds to the listener.

4. (A)

(A) is correct. A heterogeneous mixture is any nonuniform mixture, and the parts of soil are distributed unevenly.

(B) is incorrect. Salt water is a homogeneous mixture in which the salt in uniformly distributed.

(C) is incorrect. Steel is a homogeneous mixture of iron and other elements, usually carbon.

(D) is incorrect. Air is a homogeneous mixture of many different molecules, including oxygen and nitrogen gases and water vapor.

(E) is incorrect. Vinegar is a homogeneous mixture of water and acetic acid.

5. (A)

(A) is correct. Only the first two planets, Mercury and Venus, lack moons.

(B) is incorrect. Earth has one moon.

(C) is incorrect. Jupiter has many moons.

(D) is incorrect. Saturn has many moons.

(E) is incorrect. Like Mercury, Venus lacks a moon.

6. (E)

(A) is incorrect. Plastic is an insulator. Insulators block the flow of heat from one object to another.

(B) is incorrect. Rubber is an insulator.

(C) is incorrect. Porcelain is an insulator.

(D) is incorrect. Air is an insulator.

(E) is correct. Aluminum is a good thermal conductor because heat energy can move easily through it.

7. (A)

(A) is correct. Conduction is the transfer of heat from the contact of a solid or liquid to another solid or liquid.

(B) is incorrect. Convection is the transfer of heat from particle to particle within a fluid or gas during circular motion.

(C) is incorrect. Radiation occurs as energy transfer in the form of a wave when a very hot object, such as the sun, emits a certain wavelength.

(D) is incorrect. Sublimation occurs when a solid changes state directly to a gas without reaching a liquid state first.

(E) is incorrect. Evaporation occurs when a liquid changes state to a gas.

8. **(C)**

(A) is incorrect. The two charges are both negative and so will interact, causing them to move.

(B) is incorrect. The charges are both negative, so they will repel, not attract, each other.

(C) is correct. The two charges are both negative, so they will repel each other and move apart.

(D) is incorrect. The two charges would move in the same direction only if they were being acted on by an outside force.

(E) is incorrect. The charges' movement will not be random: it will be determined by the magnitude of the charges and the distance between them.

9. **(A)**

(A) is correct. Strong acids break apart into their constituent ions immediately when placed in water.

(B) is incorrect. Strong acids may donate only one proton.

(C) is incorrect. A substance with a pH of 7 is neutral; a strong acid has a pH close to 1.

(D) is incorrect. A strong acid ionizes easily, releasing protons.

(E) is incorrect. A strong acid does not need to contain a metal.

10. **(C)**

(A) is incorrect. Protons are positively charged particles in the nucleus.

(B) is incorrect. Neutrons are particles in the nucleus that have no charge.

(C) is correct. Electrons are negatively charged particles in an atom; electrons orbit the nucleus.

(D) is incorrect. Ions are atoms that have lost or gained electrons and have a charge.

(E) is incorrect. The nucleus is comprised of an atom's protons and neutrons.

11. **(E)**

(A) is incorrect. Temperature generally decreases with increasing altitude in the troposphere.

(B) is incorrect. Pressure generally decreases with increasing altitude in the troposphere.

(C) is incorrect. Density generally decreases with increasing altitude in the troposphere, as the molecules are spread farther apart with increasing elevation.

(D) is incorrect. Temperature, pressure, and density do not increase as altitude increases.

(E) is correct. Temperature, pressure, and density all decrease as altitude increases.

12. **(C)**

(A) is incorrect. Stratus clouds are associated with light and continuous precipitation and are composed of water droplets.

(B) is incorrect. Cumulonimbus clouds are large, anvil-shaped clouds associated with thunderstorms and are composed mainly of water droplets.

(C) is correct. Cirrus clouds are associated with fair weather and are composed entirely of ice crystals.

(D) is incorrect. Nimbostratus clouds are dark, low-level clouds associated with light to moderate rain; they may contain ice particles in addition to water droplets.

(E) is incorrect. Stratocumulus clouds are associated with light precipitation and are often seen at the front end of larger storms.

13. (C)

(A) is incorrect. Mass is the amount of matter in an object. Weight is a measure of the gravitational pull on an object. Weight changes in space, but mass does not.

(B) is incorrect. Weight is created by gravitational pull, not mass.

(C) is correct. Weight is a force created by gravitational pull.

(D) is incorrect. The surface area or size of an object does not indicate the mass of that object.

(E) is incorrect. Because weight is caused by gravitational pull, its value changes depending on the nearest large body. For example, the weight of an object on the moon is less than its weight on Earth.

14. (B)

(A) is incorrect. Compaction is the process through which sediment is compressed to create sedimentary rock.

(B) is correct. Heat and pressure change the composition of sedimentary rock to create metamorphic rock.

(C) is incorrect. Crystallization occurs when hot flowing magma develops mineral crystals as it cools and hardens.

(D) is incorrect. Weathering is the process responsible for the wearing away of rocks, minerals, and soils.

(E) is incorrect. Erosion is the process through which the sediment produced by weathering is carried to a new location.

15. (C)

(A) is incorrect. A thermometer measures temperature.

(B) is incorrect. A graduated cylinder measures volume.

(C) is correct. A balance measures mass.

(D) is incorrect. An ammeter is used to measure current in a circuit.

(E) is incorrect. A ruler is used to measure length.

16. (C)

(A) is incorrect. Cave formation is an example of chemical weathering. Chemical weathering involves a chemical change.

(B) is incorrect. Rusting is an example of chemical weathering.

(C) is correct. Mechanical weathering involves breaking a substance down without changing the composition of the substance.

(D) is incorrect. Bananas turning brown is an example of a chemical change.

(E) is incorrect. Feldspar's reaction with water to produce clay is a chemical change.

17. (E)

(A) is incorrect. Acids have a pH between 0 and 7.

(B) is incorrect. Acids have a pH between 0 and 7.

(C) is incorrect. Acids have a pH between 0 and 7.

(D) is incorrect. A substance with a pH of 7 is neutral.

(E) is correct. Bases have a pH between 7 and 14.

18. (B)

(A) is incorrect. The exosphere is the outermost layer of the earth's atmosphere.

(B) is correct. The lithosphere is the top layer of the earth's surface.

(C) is incorrect. The atmosphere refers to the layer of gases that surrounds the earth.

(D) is incorrect. The biosphere is the part of Earth where life exists; the biosphere includes the atmosphere, the oceans, and the life-supporting areas above and below Earth's surface.

(E) is incorrect. The asthenosphere lies under the lithosphere.

19. (D)

(A) is incorrect. Positive and negative charge is neither created nor destroyed. No particle can change its charge.

(B) is incorrect. Electrons, not protons, move to create current.

(C) is incorrect. Voltage sources are sources of electric potential. They do not store electrons.

(D) is correct. The valence electrons are the outermost and most loosely held electrons. They are more likely to move in a conducting material.

(E) is incorrect. While valence electrons are important for chemical bonding, these chemical bonds do not play a role in carrying current.

20. **(C)**

(A) is incorrect. Water can generate hydropower, which is a renewable energy source.

(B) is incorrect. Wind is a renewable energy source.

(C) is correct. Coal is nonrenewable because once coal is burned, it cannot be quickly replaced.

(D) is incorrect. Solar energy is a renewable energy source.

(E) is incorrect. Geothermal energy is a renewable energy source.

TABLE READING

1.	(B)	21.	(C)
2.	(D)	22.	(D)
3.	(E)	23.	(A)
4.	(B)	24.	(B)
5.	(B)	25.	(E)
6.	(E)	26.	(B)
7.	(C)	27.	(B)
8.	(D)	28.	(D)
9.	(B)	29.	(A)
10.	(B)	30.	(E)
11.	(D)	31.	(D)
12.	(D)	32.	(A)
13.	(C)	33.	(B)
14.	(E)	34.	(E)
15.	(C)	35.	(C)
16.	(D)	36.	(C)
17.	(C)	37.	(A)
18.	(E)	38.	(B)
19.	(C)	39.	(D)
20.	(E)	40.	(E)

1.	(A)	level flight	banking right	north
2.	(C)	climbing	banking left	east
3.	(B)	level flight	banking right	south
4.	(B)	climbing	banking left	west
5.	(A)	level flight	banking left	east
6.	(C)	level flight	banking left	north
7.	(B)	descending	no bank	southwest
8.	(D)	descending	banking right	southwest
9.	(C)	level flight	banking left	south
10.	(B)	level flight	banking right	east
11.	(A)	descending	banking left	west
12.	(D)	descending	no bank	east
13.	(A)	descending	banking right	southeast
14.	(B)	climbing	banking left	north
15.	(A)	descending	banking right	west
16.	(D)	descending	banking left	southeast
17.	(C)	descending	no bank	west
18.	(B)	climbing	no bank	west
19.	(D)	climbing	banking right	west
20.	(D)	descending	no bank	southeast
21.	(C)	climbing	no bank	east
22.	(B)	climbing	banking right	northeast
23.	(A)	climbing	banking right	north
24.	(B)	level flight	banking right	north
25.	(C)	level flight	banking eight	east

BLOCK COUNTING

1. (C)
2. (A)
3. (A)
4. (B)
5. (D)
6. (E)
7. (D)
8. (B)
9. (E)
10. (B)
11. (B)
12. (E)
13. (C)
14. (B)
15. (A)

16. (D)
17. (A)
18. (A)
19. (C)
20. (B)
21. (B)
22. (E)
23. (A)
24. (B)
25. (C)
26. (D)
27. (D)
28. (C)
29. (C)
30. (B)

1. **(B)**

    (A) is incorrect. The rudder does not extend outward, and it is controlled by the foot pedals, not by the cyclic.

    (B) is correct. The cyclic does not control the rudder.

    (C) is incorrect. The rudder does not shift from input to the cyclic.

    (D) is incorrect. The rudder does not shift from input to the cyclic.

    (E) is incorrect. The rudder does not move up and down.

2. **(B)**

    (A) is incorrect. The ailerons affect roll along the longitudinal axis of the aircraft, but so do the spoilers, so this is not the best answer.

    (B) is correct. Both the ailerons and the spoilers affect the roll of an aircraft, so this is the best answer.

    (C) is incorrect. The elevators control pitch along the lateral axis of the aircraft.

    (D) is incorrect. The rudder affects the vertical axis of the aircraft.

    (E) is incorrect. Neither component affects the roll of an aircraft.

3. **(B)**

    (A) is incorrect. This climb is used to clear obstacles in the flight path.

    (B) is correct. This climb is used to reach the greatest altitude over a given amount of time, requiring maximum power.

    (C) is incorrect. This is not a type of climb.

    (D) is incorrect. This climb is not used with maximum power.

    (E) is incorrect. This is not a type of climb.

4. **(B)**

    (A) is incorrect. The coaxial rotor system cancels torque effect by using counter-rotating rotor heads.

    (B) is correct. The NOTAR design uses a ducted fan to vector air out of the tail to cancel torque effect.

    (C) is incorrect. The tandem rotor system cancels torque effect through the use of counter-rotating rotor heads.

    (D) is incorrect. The term *semi-monocoque* refers to a fuselage type that utilizes longitudinal reinforcement to add strength.

    (E) is incorrect. The skids are used as landing gear for rotary-wing aircraft.

5. **(E)**

    (A) is incorrect. The airflow over and around the extended wings causes an increase in drag.

    (B) is incorrect. On an approach to land, since airspeed is decreased, maximum lift is required to keep the aircraft airborne until touchdown.

    (C) is incorrect. An aircraft must decrease airspeed when approaching to land.

    (D) is incorrect. Although high drag is created, an increase in airspeed is not created.

    (E) is correct. Since airspeed is decreased, maximum lift is required plus high drag to slow the aircraft.

6. **(B)**

    (A) is incorrect. Increasing the throttle increases manifold pressure.

    (B) is correct. This decreases the manifold pressure, which in turn increases rpm.

    (C) is incorrect. Cyclic movement does not affect manifold pressure.

    (D) is incorrect. This increases manifold pressure and decreases rpm.

    (E) is incorrect. This decreases rpm and manifold pressure.

7. **(A)**

(A) is correct. Weight, lift, thrust, and drag must be in balance in order to hover.

(B) is incorrect. An effective translational lift results from increased efficiency of the main rotor system as directional flight is established.

(C) is incorrect. Dissymmetry of lift is the unequal lifting of forces created by the advancing and retreating blades.

(D) is incorrect. Gyroscopic precession is when a force input is applied yet the force output is felt 90 degrees later in the plane of rotation.

(E) is incorrect. Autorotation is when the rotor blades are driven by relative wind rather than by the aircraft's powerplant.

8. **(B)**

(A) is incorrect. This would increase or decrease the pitch, not move the ball to the center.

(B) is correct. The foot pedals control the rudder, which moves the aircraft left or right.

(C) is incorrect. The pitot tube measures airspeed and has no impact on changing the pitch of an aircraft.

(D) is incorrect. This would only adjust the barometric pressure for an altitude indicator.

(E) is incorrect. This would increase power from the engine; it would not change the direction to center the ball.

9. **(D)**

(A) is incorrect. The fuselage includes the crew, passenger, and cargo areas.

(B) is incorrect. The tail section is separate from the landing gear section.

(C) is incorrect. These are not part of the tail section, the empennage.

(D) is correct. The tail section is known as the empennage.

(E) is incorrect. The wings are not part of the empennage.

10. **(D)**

(A) is incorrect. The teeter hinge allows the blades to flap.

(B) is incorrect. The swashplate allows for directional movement of the aircraft.

(C) is incorrect. The ducted fan is a component of the NOTAR aircraft design.

(D) is correct. The tail boom is a structural component that supports the tail rotor assembly.

(E) is incorrect. The skids are used as landing gear for rotary-wing aircraft.

11. **(C)**

(A) is incorrect. The flaps are part of the secondary flight control system.

(B) is incorrect. The leading edge devices are also part of the secondary flight control system.

(C) is correct. The rudder is part of the primary flight control system.

(D) is incorrect. The spoilers are part of the secondary flight control system too.

(E) is incorrect. The trim tabs are also part of the secondary flight control system.

12. **(B)**

(A) is incorrect. Do not halve the degree of variation.

(B) is correct. "East is least, west is best." The adjustment is a 15-degree west variation.

(C) is incorrect. Do not take the difference from 360 degrees to determine variation.

(D) is incorrect. "East is least, west is best." Subtract for an easterly variation, and add for a westerly variation.

(E) is incorrect. Do not take the difference from 360 degrees to determine variation.

13. (E)

(A) is incorrect. The induced flow will not move horizontally.

(B) is incorrect. The induced flow will not move backward.

(C) is incorrect. The induced flow will not move parallel to the plane of rotation.

(D) is incorrect. The induced flow will not move to the right.

(E) is correct. Induced flow, also known as downwash, moves vertically up through the rotor system.

14. (E)

(A) is incorrect. Compasses are used when the heading indicator fails.

(B) is incorrect. These do not correct in-flight compass reading errors.

(C) is incorrect. This compass has inherent errors.

(D) is incorrect. These do not correct in-flight compass reading errors.

(E) is correct. This compass was developed to reduce reading errors.

15. (A)

(A) is correct. Aircraft in distress always have the right-of-way over other aircraft.

(B) is incorrect. Hot-air balloons do not always have the right-of-way.

(C) is incorrect. Jets do not always have the right-of-way.

(D) is incorrect. Powered parachutes do not always have the right-of-way.

(E) is incorrect. The right-of-way protocol applies to both controlled and uncontrolled airspaces.

16. (E)

(A) is incorrect. This instrument displays the altitude.

(B) is incorrect. This instrument displays the heading (degrees) of the aircraft.

(C) is incorrect. This instrument is used as a backup if the heading indicator fails.

(D) is incorrect. This instrument displays the heading of the aircraft.

(E) is correct. This instrument will indeed display if the aircraft is in a climb, in a descent, or in level flight.

17. (D)

(A) is incorrect. Aircraft cannot fly with contaminated fuel.

(B) is incorrect. Aircraft manufacturers deliver their aircraft with the tanks empty.

(C) is incorrect. This fuel is usable fuel.

(D) is correct. This is fuel that cannot be used and cannot be drained from the tanks.

(E) is incorrect. Fuel spills are not considered unusable fuel as such.

18. (A)

(A) is correct. The aircraft moves forward when the cyclic is pushed forward.

(B) is incorrect. The aircraft will not move backward.

(C) is incorrect. The aircraft will not spin in circles.

(D) is incorrect. The aircraft will not turn left.

(E) is incorrect. The nose of the aircraft will not pitch up.

19. (C)

(A) is incorrect. The cyclic controls the pitch and roll axis of the aircraft.

(B) is incorrect. The collective changes the pitch of the blades simultaneously.

(C) is correct. The tail rotor pedals control the yaw axis of the aircraft.

(D) is incorrect. Translating tendency causes a rotary-wing aircraft to drift laterally due to tail rotor thrust.

(E) is incorrect. The throttle maintains the engine within optimal flight parameters.

20. (A)

(A) is correct. Absolute altitude is measured above ground level (AGL).

(B) is incorrect. Density altitude is pressure altitude modified for a nonstandard temperature.

(C) is incorrect. Indicated altitude is the current altitude displayed on an altimeter.

(D) is incorrect. Pressure altitude is an indicated altitude determined with a standard atmosphere level setting of 29.92 Hg.

(E) is incorrect. True altitude is measured from mean sea level (MSL).

92106553R00087

Made in the USA
Columbia, SC
23 March 2018